SOME PERSONAL LETTERS OF HERMAN MELVILLE
AND
A BIBLIOGRAPHY

Norman Melville

SOME PERSONAL LETTERS
OF HERMAN MELVILLE

AND

A BIBLIOGRAPHY

BY

MEADE MINNIGERODE

Select Bibliographies Reprint Series

BOOKS FOR LIBRARIES PRESS
FREEPORT, NEW YORK

First Published 1922
Reprinted 1969

LIBRARY OF CONGRESS CATALOG CARD NUMBER:
78-75511

PRINTED IN THE UNITED STATES OF AMERICA

TO
WILLIAM LYON PHELPS

" . . . Herman Melville is undoubtedly an original thinker, and boldly and unreservedly expresses his opinions, often in a way that irresistibly startles and enchains the interest of the reader. He possesses amazing powers of expression; he can be terse, copious, eloquent, brilliant, imaginative, poetical, satirical, pathetic, at will. He is never stupid, never dull; but alas! he is often mystical and unintelligible, *not* from any inability to express himself, for his writing is pure, manly English, and a child can always understand what he *says*—but the ablest critic cannot always tell what he really *means*. . . .

"Such is Herman Melville! A man of whom America has reason to be proud, with all his faults; and, if he does not eventually rank as one of her greatest giants in literature, it will not be owing to any lack of innate genius, but solely to his own incorrigible perversion of his rare and lofty gifts."

Dublin University Magazine.

HERMAN MELVILLE

Born, 6 Pearl Street, New York City,
August 1, 1819.
Died, 104 East 26th Street, New York City,
September 28, 1891.

"Call me Ishmael. Some years ago—
never mind how long precisely—having little or no money in my purse, and nothing
particular to interest me on shore, I thought
I would sail about a little, and see the watery
part of the world. It is a way I have of
driving off the spleen, and regulating the
circulation. . . ."

Moby-Dick.

CONTENTS

[xi]

ILLUSTRATIONS

PART I

SOME PERSONAL LETTERS

INTRODUCTION

FAME has returned to Herman Melville after seventy years.

Mr. Masefield has spoken. Mr. Weaver has written. First edition copies of Melville's works have been removed from the dusty limbo of unconsidered counters and placed in aristocratic company upon the high-priced shelves of bibliophiles. Soon, in the land of his birth, it will be possible to mention his name in public gatherings without explanatory identification.

These things may possibly compensate his spirit for forty years of neglect during his lifetime, followed by thirty years of oblivion after his death. In the meantime, the same country that ignored him, living—the same native city that forgot that he had not yet died, until it discovered that he had—will now tardily honor him with widespread curiosity.

In this volume are offered—many of them, it is believed, for the first time—a score of letters written by Herman Melville between the years 1846-1860, that is to say during the most productive years of his life, and the period which saw the writing of his disastrous *Pierre*. The let-

[3]

ters were written to his close friend, Evert Duyckinck, editor of *The Literary World* (1847-
1853) in New York City, and are to be found
in the Duyckinck Collection of Manuscripts in the
New York Public Library. They contain references to Melville's own books, autobiographical
data of absorbing interest, comments on literary
personalities of the day, and occasionally a de-
scriptive passage of great beauty.

Whatever the final estimate of Melville as a
writer, whatever the ultimate judgment passed
upon him as a mystic, an eccentric, a recluse, and
a wilfully perverted genius—the author of *Mardi*
and *Moby-Dick,* the perpetrator of *Pierre*—in
these letters, at least, one finds an utterly different
Melville. A cheerful, whimsical Melville; a
lover of company, and of the good things of life;
a gay, ironical fellow, aiming his witty shafts at
the gods; a turbulent *enfant terrible* at times, with
his impudent personal pen, and yet a sensitive
soul, recoiling from criticism and abuse; a hot-
headed proclaimer of truth; a vivid, warm-
hearted, gentle, friendly, impulsive personality;
and for several years a patient sufferer from a
great infirmity.

After reading the letters from Arrowhead,
who would not wish that he might have made a
way through the New England snowdrifts to
Melville's door, to share the comfort of his fire
and the warmth of his welcome,—a pathetically

[4]

eager welcome, one almost suspects,—feed his horse and visit his cow, and furnish some interest, however inadequate, to his evening of enforced idleness caused by that twilight of his eyes of which he speaks. . . .

The original orthography, etc., of the letters has been preserved throughout.

M. M.

May 2, 1922.

I

A MAN'S WORK

THE letter given below, while of later date than some which follow in this volume, is placed first in the collection for the reason that it furnishes a striking revelation of Melville's attitude towards a man's work, and of the world's appreciation of that work.

In the light of Melville's subsequent career as an author, the first paragraph is amazingly prophetic, although in his case the "steam of adulation" did not begin to rise until some thirty years after the sexton had completed his task. It is interesting to note the transition of Melville's thought from the general to the particular in this paragraph.

The letter was written from Boston, on April 5, 1849, a few days before the publication of *Mardi*. Melville was not quite thirty at the time, and had achieved a very considerable success with his first two books, *Typee* and *Omoo*.

In view of the fact that certain critics in the past have ventured to put forward the theory that Melville's mind became impaired, in explanation of the obscurities encountered in some of his later work, the paragraph concerning insanity is of special interest. The Mr. Hoffman referred to was one of the editors of *The Literary World*.

"Dear Duyckinck . . . All ambitious authors should have ghosts capable of revisiting the world, to snuff up the steam of adulation, which begins to rise strengthening as the Sexton throws his last shovelfull on him —Down goes his body and up flies his name. . . .

"Poor Hoffman . . . This going mad of a friend or acquaintance comes straight home to every man who feels his soul in him, which but few men do. For in all of us lodges the same fuel to light the same fire. And he who has never felt, momentarily, what madness is has but a mouthful of brains. What sort of sensation permanent madness is may be very well imagined just as we imagine how we felt when we were infants, tho' we can not recall it. In both conditions we are irresponsible and riot like gods without fear of fate—It is the climax of a wild night of revelry when the blood has been transmuted into brandy—But if we prate much of this, why we shall be illustrating our own proposition. . . .

"Would that a man could do something

and then say It is finished—not that one thing only, but all others—that he has reached his uttermost and can never exceed it. But live and push—tho' we put one leg forward ten miles is no reason the other must lag behind—no, that must again distance the other—and so we go till we get cramp and die. . . .

H. Melville."

II

TYPEE AND OMOO

IN January, 1841, when he was twenty-one
years old, Melville shipped before the mast
—his second venture of this nature—aboard the
whaler *Acushnet,* out of New Bedford. A vessel
of 359 tons, owned by Bradford Fuller and Company, commanded by Captain Pease.

Of her condition six months later Melville
writes in the opening paragraph of *Typee:*

"Six months at sea! Yes, reader, as I
live, six months out of sight of land; cruising
after the sperm-whale beneath the scorching
sun of the Line, and tossed on the billows of
the wide-rolling Pacific—the sky above, the
sea around, and nothing else! Weeks and
weeks ago our fresh provisions were all ex-
hausted. There is not a sweet potatoe left;
not a single yam. Those glorious bunches of
banannas which once decorated our stern and
quarter-deck, have, alas, disappeared! and
the delicious oranges which hung suspended

from our tops and stays—they, too, are gone! Yes, they are all departed and there is nothing left us but salt-horse and sea-biscuit."

Again, in a later chapter, he writes:

"The usage on board of her was tyrannical; the sick had been inhumanly neglected; the provisions had been doled out in scanty allowance; and her cruises were unreasonably protracted. The captain was the author of these abuses; it was in vain to think that he would either remedy them, or alter his conduct, which was arbitrary and violent in the extreme. His prompt reply to all complaints and remonstrances was—the butt end of a handspike, so convincingly administered as effectually to silence the aggrieved party."

A few days after the ship arrived in Nukuheva Bay, in the Marquesas, Melville deserted, together with a shipmate, Toby. After incredible adventures and hardships, they found themselves prisoner-guests of the cannibal natives of the Valley of Typee. Toby succeeded in escaping after a brief sojourn, but Melville remained for four months in the Valley, where he seems to have enjoyed a number of highly entertaining experiences as the guest of Kory-Kory and Tinor, and the fascinating Fayaway. In fact, in Typee, Mel-

ville did as the Typees do, except that he refused
to be tattooed and avoided being devoured.

He was finally rescued, in a spirited running
fight, by an Australian whaler which he calls the
Julia; a sweet ship which he describes as follows
in *Omoo:*

> "On approaching, she turned out to be a
> small, slatternly looking craft, her hull and
> spars a dingy black, rigging all slack and
> bleached nearly white, and everything denot-
> ing an ill state of affairs aboard. . . .
> "She was a small barque of a beautiful
> model, something more than two hundred
> tons, Yankee-built and very old. Fitted for
> a privateer out of a New England port dur-
> ing the war of 1812, she had been captured
> at sea by a British cruiser, and, after seeing
> all sorts of service, was at last employed as
> a government packet in the Australian seas.
> Being condemned, however, about two years
> previous, she was purchased at auction by a
> house in Sydney, who, after some slight re-
> pairs, dispatched her on the present voyage.
> "Notwithstanding the repairs, she was
> still in a miserable plight. The lower masts
> were said to be unsound; the standing rig-
> ging was much worn; and, in some places,
> even the bulwarks were quite rotten. Still,
> she was tolerably tight, and but little more

than the ordinary pumping of a morning served to keep her free."

A capital ship for an ocean trip, in other words! Melville continues, with his bland realism:

" . . . Concerning the cockroaches, there was an extraordinary phenomenon, for which none of us could ever account.

"Every night they had a jubilee. The first symptom was an unusual clustering and humming among the swarms lining the beams overhead, and the inside of the sleeping-places. This was succeeded by a prodigious coming and going on the part of those living out of sight. Presently they all came forth; the larger sort racing over the chests and planks; winged monsters darting to and fro in the air; and the small fry buzzing in heaps almost in a state of fusion."

There are also some observations concerning rats. In Tahiti the entire crew mutinied and went ashore, where the *Julia* left them.

In 1845, Melville wrote an account of his experiences in the Marquesas in *Typee,* published in 1846. This was followed in 1847 by *Omoo,* continuing the story after his escape from the cannibal valley. The books made a sensation in more ways than one. The publishers of *Typee* made much of:

[13]

" . . . cannibal banquets . . . savage woodlands guarded by horrible idols, *heathenish
rites, and human sacrifices.*"

The missionaries made much of certain other
features of the tales; reviewers emptied inkwells
over them; Melville was the main topic of con-
versation in every gathering and around every
dinner table. And a great many people refused
to believe one word of *Typee*.

One does not need to be the author of a dis-
credited true story to appreciate Melville's annoy-
ance, and the consequent delight manifest in the
following letter, written on July 3, 1846, from
Lansingburg:

"There was a spice of civil scepticism in
your manner, my dear Sir, when we were
conversing together the other day about
'Typee'—what will the politely incredulous
Mr. Duyckinck now say to the true Toby's
having turned up in Buffalo, and written a
letter to the Commercial Advertiser of that
place, vouching for the truth of all that part
(which has been considered the most extraordinary part) of the narrative, where he is
made to figure.

"Give ear then, oh ye of little faith—especially thou man of the Evangelist—and hear
what Toby has to say for himself.—

"Seriously, my dear Sir, this resurrection

of Toby from the dead—this strange bring-
ing together of two such places as Typee and
Buffalo, is really very curious.—It can not
but settle the question of the book's genuine-
ness. The article in the C. A. with the letter
of Toby can not possibly be gainsaid in any
conceivable way—therefore I think they
[*erased*] it ought to be pushed into circulation. I doubt not but that many papers
will copy it—Mr. Duyckinck might say a
word or two on the subject which would tell.
—The paper I allude to is of the 1st inst.

"I have written Toby a letter and expect to
see him soon and hear the sequel of the book
I have written (How strangely that sounds!)

"Bye the bye, since people have always
manifested so much concern for 'poor Toby,'
what do you think of writing an account of
what befell him in escaping from the island
—should the adventure prove to be of suffi-
cient interest?—I should value your opinion
very highly on this subject.

"I began with the intention of tracing a
short note—I have come near writing a long
letter.

"Believe me, my dear Sir,

Very truly yours,

Herman Melville.

* * * * *

"P. S. No. 2.   Possibly the letter of Toby
might by some silly ones be regarded as a
hoax—to set you right on that point, altho'
I only saw the letter last night for the first—
I will tell you that it alludes to things that no
human being could have heard of except
Toby. Besides the Editor seems to have seen
him."

This letter refers of course to the reappear-
ance of Melville's shipmate Toby, Richard
Tobias Greene, whose letter to the Buffalo *Commercial Advertiser,* together with the Editor's
comment, are given below. The word *mortarkee*
in Typee signifies "good!"

"How strangely things turn up!
"One of the most curious and entertaining books published last season was a work
entitled 'Typee, a residence in the Marquesas.' We read it with great interest, but the
impression it left on the mind was that the
incidents and mode of life it described were
too extraordinary, and too much at variance
with what is known of savage life, to be true,
and that like the fabled *Atlantis* or the travels of *Gaudentio di Lucca* though without
their philosophical pretension, it was the off-
spring of a lively inventive fancy, rather
than a veritable narrative of facts. This
impression, we believe, was very general.

[16]

The readers of *Typee* therefore can imagine, and will share, our surprise, at hearing that here in Buffalo, is a credible witness of the truth of some of the most extraordinary incidents narrated in the book. Toby, the companion of Mr. Melville in the flight from the whale ship and whom in his book he supposes to be dead, is now living in this city, following the business of a house and sign painter. His father is a respectable farmer in the town of Darien, Genesee Co. We received from Toby this morning the subjoined communication. His verbal statements correspond in all essential particulars with those made by Mr. Melville respecting their joint adventures and from the assurances we have received in regard to Toby's character, we have no reason to doubt his word. His turning up here is a strange verification of a very strange and as has been hitherto deemed an almost incredible book:

" 'To the Editor of the Buffalo *Commercial Advertiser:*

" 'In the *New York Evangelist* I chanced to see a notice of a new publication in two parts called "Typee, a residence in the Marquesas" by Herman Melville. In the book he speaks of his comrade in misfortune "Toby" who left him so mysteriously and whom he supposed had been killed by the

Happar natives. The *Evangelist* speaks
rather disparagingly of the book as being
too romantic to be true, and as being too
severe on the missionaries. But to my object: I am the true and veritable "Toby" yet
living, and I am happy to testify to the entire accuracy of the work so long as I was
with Melville, who makes me figure so
largely in it. I have not heard of Melville,
or "Tommo," since I left him on the Island,
and likewise supposed him to be dead; and
not knowing where a letter would find him,
and being anxious to know where he is, and
to tell him my "yarn" and compare "log"
books, I have concluded to ask you to insert
this notice, and inform him of my yet being
alive and to ask you to request New York,
Albany, and Boston papers to publish this
notice so that it may reach him. My true
name is Richard Greene, and I have the scar
on my head which I received from the Happar spear and which came near killing me.
I left Melville and fell in with an Irishman
who had resided on the island for some time
and who assisted me in returning to the ship,
and who faithfully promised me to go and
bring Melville to our ship next day, which
he never did, his only object being money. I
gave him five dollars to get me on board, but
could not return to Melville. I sailed to New

[18]

Zealand and thence home; and I request Melville to send me his address if this should chance to meet his eye. *"Mortarkee"* was the word I used when I heard of his being alive.

Toby.' "

Melville's letter also contains probably the first reference to a projected sequel to *Typee,* which was shortly after incorporated in the Revised Edition.

2

On July 28, 1846, Melville wrote as follows:

"You remember you said something about anticipating the piracy that might be perpetrated on the 'Sequel,' by publishing an extract or two from it—which you said you would attend to—I meant to speak to you again about it, but forgot to do so. . . . I take this to be a matter of some little moment.

"The *Revised* (Expurgated? — Odious word!) Edition of 'Typee' ought to be duly announced—and as the matter (in one respect) is a little delicate, I am happy that the literary tact of Mr. Duyckinck will be exerted on the occasion. . . .

Very faithfully yours

Herman Melville."

[19]

The Revised Edition appeared in due course, and Melville's suggestion that what was really intended was an Expurgated Edition was amply corroborated. Under cover of a revision, involving the omission of the Appendix and the addition of "The Story of Toby," some drastic changes were made in the text, which are noticed in full in Part II of this volume. One need here only examine a few of them to appreciate Melville's disgust at the enforced alterations in his manuscript.

The first set of expurgations have to do with Melville's references to missionaries. This is undoubtedly the delicate matter of which he speaks in his letter. Melville disliked missionaries, and did not hesitate to state the fact, together with his reasons.

In the Preface to the original edition he says:

"There are a few passages in the ensuing chapters which may be thought to bear rather hard upon a reverend order of men, the account of whose proceedings in different quarters of the globe—transmitted to us through their own hands—very generally, and often very deservedly, receives high commendation. Such passages will be found, however, to be based upon facts admitting of no contradiction, and which have come immediately under the writer's cognisance. The conclusions deduced from these facts are unavoidable, and in stating them the author has been influenced by no feeling of animosity, either to the individuals themselves or to that glorious cause which has not always been served by the proceedings of some of its advocates."

Elsewhere in the original text he writes:

" . . . As a religious solemnity, however, it had not at all corresponded with the horrible description of Polynesian worship which we have received in some published narratives, and especially in those accounts of the evangelized islands with which the missionaries have favored us. Did not the sacred character of these persons render the purity of their intentions unquestionable, I should certainly be led to suppose that they had exaggerated the evils of Paganism, in order to enhance the merit of their own disinterested labors."

And again, speaking of the natives:

"Better will it be for them for ever to remain the happy and innocent heathens and barbarians that they now are, than, like the wretched inhabitants of the Sandwich Islands, to enjoy the mere name of Chris-

[21]

tians without experiencing any of the vital operations of true religion whilst, at the same time, they are made the victims of the worst vices and evils of civilization."

Moreover, in the original text, this passage is to be found:

"An intrepid missionary, undaunted by the ill-success that had attended all previous endeavors to conciliate the savages, and believing much in the efficacy of female influence, introduced among them his young and beautiful wife, the first white woman who had ever visited their shores. The islanders at first gazed in mute admiration at so unusual a prodigy, and seemed inclined to regard it as some new divinity. But after a short time, becoming familiar with its charming aspect, and jealous of the folds which encircled its form, they sought to pierce the sacred veil of calico in which it was enshrined, and in the gratification of their curiosity so far overstepped the limits of good breeding as deeply to offend the lady's sense of decorum. Her sex once ascertained, their idolatry was changed into contempt. . . . To the horror of her affectionate spouse, she was stripped of her garments, and given to understand that she could no longer carry on her deceits with impunity. The gentle dame was not sufficiently evangelized to endure this, and, fearful of further improprieties, she forced her husband to relinquish his undertaking. . . ."

To say nothing of:

"Look at Honolulu, the metropolis of the Sandwich Islands!—A community of disinterested merchants, and devoted self-exiled heralds of the Cross, located on the very spot that twenty years ago was defiled by the presence of idolatry. What a subject for an eloquent Bible-meeting orator! Nor has such an opportunity for a display of missionary rhetoric been allowed to pass by unimproved!

"But when these philanthropists send us such glowing accounts of one half of their labors, why does their modesty restrain them from publishing the other half of the good they have wrought?—Not until I visited Honolulu was I aware of the fact that the small remnant of the natives had been civilized into draught horses, and evangelized into beasts of burden. But so it is. They have been literally broken into the traces, and are harnessed to the vehicles of their spiritual instructors like so many dumb brutes!

[23]

"Among a multitude of similar exhibitions that I saw, I shall never forget a robust, red-faced, and very lady-like personage, a missionary's spouse, who day after day for months took her regular airings in a little go-cart drawn by two of the islanders. . . ."

And also the following:

"The republican missionaries of Oahu cause to be gazetted in the Court Journal, published at Honolulu, the most trivial movements of 'his gracious majesty' King Kammehammaha III., and 'their highnesses the princes of the blood royal.'—And who is his 'gracious majesty,' and what the quality of this 'blood royal?'—His 'gracious majesty' is a fat, lazy-looking blockhead, with as little character as power. He has lost the noble traits of the barbarian, without acquiring the redeeming graces of a civilized being; and, although a member of the Hawaiian Temperance Society, is a most inveterate dram-drinker."

These statements aroused a tempest of denials and invective aimed at Melville, who, in the words of one reviewer, was "a prejudiced, incompetent, and truthless witness," and were all omitted from the Revised Edition.

The second set of expurgations must have

annoyed Melville still more, for they were made obligatory by the shocked sensibilities of the day. In referring to the missionaries Melville had injured the feelings of a group of individuals who promptly retorted that he was a liar; in these other passages he had offended the sense of propriety of the community which promptly assailed him with blue pencils.

On the very first page it became necessary to delete the following no doubt extremely insulting passage:

> "Oh! ye state-room sailors, who make so much ado about a fourteen-days' passage across the Atlantic; who so pathetically relate the privations and hardships of the sea, where, after a day of breakfasting, lunching, dining off five courses, chatting, playing whist, and drinking champaign-punch, it was your hard lot to be shut up in little cabinets of mahogany and maple, and sleep for ten hours, with nothing to disturb you but 'those good-for-nothing tars, shouting and tramping overhead'—what would ye say to our six months out of sight of land?"

After describing how the Marquesan girls had swum out to the ship and clambered aboard, the following paragraph was going just a little bit too far!

"What a sight for us bachelor sailors! how avoid so dire a temptation? For who could think of tumbling these artless creatures overboard, when they had swam miles to welcome us?"

In a description of the young Marquesan girls in swimming, the words "and revealing their naked forms to the waist" were apparently deemed entirely too graphic.

The passage which tells how Melville was massaged once a day with *aka* was robbed of the following illuminating sentence:

" . . . and most refreshing and agreeable are the juices of the aka, when applied to one's limbs by the soft palms of sweet nymphs, whose bright eyes are beaming upon you with kindness. . . ."

In relating a canoe trip with Fayaway, Melville was not allowed to state that they were "on the very best terms possible with one another," and the following remarks on dancing were forthwith obliterated:

"In good sooth, they so sway their floating forms, arch their necks, toss aloft their naked arms, and glide, and swim, and whirl, that it was almost too much for a quiet, soberminded, modest young man like myself."

[26]

The words "To be sure, there were old Marheyo and Tinor, who seemed to live together quite sociably, but for all that, I had sometimes observed a comical-looking old gentleman dressed in a suit of shabby tattooing, who appeared to be equally at home," are all that remain in the Revised Edition of the original passage which reads entertainingly:

> "To be sure, there were old Marheyo and Tinor, who seemed to have a sort of nuptial understanding with one another, but for all that, I had sometimes observed a comical-looking old gentleman dressed in a suit of shabby tattooing, who had the audacity to take various liberties with the lady, and that too in the very presence of the old warrior her husband, who looked on, as good-naturedly as if nothing was happening."

In the account of his final escape Melville said originally that he parted from Fayaway, who was "sobbing indignantly"—a word which, in the Revised Edition, was prudently changed to "convulsively."

And the following pleasant and "characteristic anecdote of the Queen of Nukuheva" was hurriedly banished from the text:

> " . . . The ship's company . . . soon arrested her Majesty's attention. She singled

out from their number an old salt, whose
bare arms and feet, and exposed breast were
covered with as many inscriptions in India
ink as the lid of an Egyptian sarcophagus.
Notwithstanding all the . . . . remonstrances
of the French officers, she immediately ap-
proached the man, and . . . gazed with
admiration at the bright blue and vermilion
pricking . . . picture their consternation,
when all at once the royal lady, eager to display the hieroglyphics on her own sweet
form, bent forward for a moment, and turning sharply round, threw up the skirts of her
mantle. . . ."

3

One of the earliest references to *Omoo* is
found in a letter dated December 8, 1846.

"My dear Mr. Duyckinck
"I arrived in town last evening from the
East. As I hinted to you some time ago I
have a new book in M.S.—Relying much
upon your literary judgement I am very desirous of getting your opinion of it and (if
you feel disposed to favor me so far) to
receive your hints.—I address you now not as
being in any way connected with Messrs.
W[*iley*] and P[*utnam*] but presume to do
so confidentially as a friend.

"In passing through town some ten days since I left the M.S. with a particular lady acquaintance of mine; at whose house I intend calling this evening to obtain it. The lady resides up town. On my way down I will stop at your residence with the M.S. and will be very much pleased to see you—if not otherwise engaged—I will call, say at 8½.

"With sincere regard

Believe me, my dear Sir,

Very truly yours,

Herman Melville."

III

AN UNPUBLISHED REVIEW

MELVILLE published a number of book reviews in *The Literary World*, notably of Cooper's *Sea Lions*, Hawthorne's *Scarlet Letter*, Parkman's *Oregon Trail*, and a new edition of Cooper's *Red Rover*. The articles are unsigned, and it is more than probable that other reviews by Melville appear in that magazine which can not now be identified.

The following letter, which shows Melville in one of his irrepressible moods, was received November 11, 1848, and contains a review which, needless to say, was never published.

"What the deuce does it mean? Here's a book positively turned wrong side out, the title page on the cover, an index to the whole in more ways than one . . .

(*Description of subject matter*)

"You have been horribly imposed upon, my dear Sir. The book is no book, but a compact bundle of wrapping paper. And as for Mr. Hart, pen and ink should instantly be taken away from that impossible (?) man, upon the same principle that pistols are withdrawn from the wight bent on suicide.

"Prayers should be offered up for him among the congregations, and Thanksgiving Day postponed until long after his 'book' is published. What great national sin have we committed to deserve this infliction.

"Seriously, Mr. Duyckinck, on my bended knees, and with tears in my eyes, deliver me from writing aught upon this crucifying Romance of Yachting.

"What has Mr. Hart done that I should publicly devour him? I bear that hapless man no malice. Then why smite him? And as for glossing over his book with a few commonplaces—*that* I can not do. The book deserves to be burnt in a fire of asafetida, and by the hand that wrote it.

"Seriously again . . . the book is an abortion, the mere trunk of a book, minus head, arm or leg. Take it back, I beseech, and get some one to cart it back to the author.

Yours sincerely,

H. M."

IV

EMERSON

THE following letter, written March 3, 1849, refers to previous correspondence concerning Emerson, and gives Melville's impressions of him after hearing him lecture. The reference to the great whale is significant. And, whatever his subsequent tendencies may have been, at this time, certainly, Melville does not appear to have been a partisan of unintelligibility.

"Nay, I do not oscillate in Emerson's rainbow, but prefer rather to hang myself in mine own halter than swing in any other man's swing. Yet I think Emerson is more than a brilliant fellow. Be his stuff begged, borrowed, or stolen, or of his own domestic manufacture he is an uncommon man.

"Swear he is a humbug—then is he no uncommon humbug. Lay it down that had not Sir Thomas Browne lived, Emerson would not have mystified—I will answer that had not Old Zach's father begot him, Old Zach would never have been the hero of Palo

Alto. The truth is that we are all sons, grandsons, or nephews or great-nephews of those who go before us. No one is his own sire.

"I was very agreeably disappointed in Mr. Emerson. I had heard of him as full of transcendentalism, myths and oracular gibberish . . . to my surprise, I found him quite intelligible, tho' to say truth, they told me that that night he was unusually plain.

"Now, there is a something about every man elevated above mediocrity, which is for the most part instantly perceptible. This I see in Mr. Emerson. And, frankly, for the sake of the argument, let us call him a fool—then had I rather be a fool than a wise man.

"I love all men who *dive*. Any fish can swim near the surface, but it takes a great whale to go down stairs five miles or more; and if he don't attain the bottom, why, all the lead in Galena can't fashion the plummit that will. I'm not talking of Mr. Emerson now, but of the whole corps of thought-divers that have been diving and coming up again with blood-shot eyes since the world began.

"I could readily see in Emerson, notwithstanding his merit, a gaping flaw. It was, the insinuation that had he lived in those days when the world was made, he might have offered some valuable suggestions. These men are all cracked right across the brow. And never will the pullers-down be able to cope with the builders-up. . . . But enough of this Plato who talks thro' his nose. . . .

"You complain that Emerson tho' a denizen of the land of gingerbread, is above munching a plain cake in company of jolly fellows, and swigging (?) off his ale like you and me. Ah, my dear Sir, that's his misfortune, not his fault. His belly, Sir, is in his chest, and his brains descend down into his neck, and offer an obstacle to a draughtful of ale or a mouthful of cake. . . . Goodbye.

H. M."

V

MARDI

ON April 14, 1849, Melville published *Mardi,* his third book. In the Preface he says of it:

> "Not long ago, having published two narratives of voyages in the Pacific, which, in many quarters, were received with incredulity, the thought occurred to me, of indeed writing a romance of Polynesian adventure, and publishing it as such; to see whether the fiction might not, possibly, be received for a verity: in some degree the reverse of my previous experience."

One encounters in this book such personages as the Chondropterygii, Little King Peepi, Donjalolo, Babbalanja, "those scamps" the Plujii, "that jolly old Lord" Borabolla. One visits the Island of Juam, "that jolly Island" Mondoldo, the Lake of Yammo, the Catacombs, Pimminee, Dominora, Porpheero, the Land of Warwicks or King-makers, and Hooloomooloo. With Taji, one sits down to dinner with five-and-twenty kings.

One discusses the hereafters of Fish, and what manner of men the Tapparians were, and Mollusca, Kings, Toad-stools, and other matters.

The book is full of marvels and portents, history, zoölogy, adventure, and philosophy. Perhaps much of it is allegory, on the other hand perhaps nearly all of it is burlesque.

" . . . most ancient of all, was a hieroglyphical Elegy on the Dumps, consisting of one thousand and one lines. . . . Then there were plenty of rare old ballads:—*King Kroko, and the Fisher Girl.* . . . And brave old chronicles . . . *The whole pedigree of the King of Kandidee, with that of his famous horse, Znorto.* . . . And Tarantula books:—*Sour milk for the young, by a dairyman.* . . . And poetical productions:—*Sonnet on the last breath of an Ephemera; The Gad-fly, and other poems* . . . and scarce old memoirs . . . *The Life of old Philo, the Philanthropist, in one chapter.* . . . And books by Chiefs and Nobles:—*on the proper manner of saluting a bosom friend* . . . *A Canto on a cough caught by my consort* . . .

"And theological works:—*Pudding for the Pious* . . . *Pickles for the Persecuted.* And long and tedious romances . . . *The King and the Cook, or the Cook and the King.* And books of voyages . . . *Franko: its*

King, Court and Tadpoles. . . . And pamphlets by retired warriors:—*Three receipts for bottling new arack; To brown bread fruit without burning.* . . ."

A great deal of it is rollicking nonsense. Not a little of it is poetry, both in prose and verse—

"Fish, Fish, we are fish with red gills:
Naught disturbs us, our blood is at zero:
We are buoyant because of our bags,
Being many, each fish is a hero.
We care not what it is, this life
That we follow, this phantom unknown:
To swim, it's exceedingly pleasant—
So swim away, making a foam. . . .

"We fish, we fish, we merrily swim,
We care not for friend, nor for foe:
Our fins are stout,
Our tails are out,
As through the seas we go . . ."

and the following, which seems to be the only direct reference in Melville's writings to the California gold rush—

"Now, northward coasting along Kolumbo's Western shore . . . and where we landed not . . . and after many, many days, we spied prow after prow, before the wind all

northward bound: sails widespread, and pad-
dles plying: scaring the fish from before
them.

" . . . But as they sped, with frantic glee,
in one long chorus thus they sang:—

"We rovers bold,
  To the land of gold,
Over bowling billows are gliding:
  Eager to toil,
  For the golden spoil,
And every hardship biding.
See! See!
Before our prow's resistless dashes,
The gold-fish fly in golden flashes!
'Neath a sun of gold,
We rovers bold,
On the golden land are gaining;
And every night,
We steer aright,
By golden stars unwaning!
All fires burn a golden glare:
No locks so bright as golden hair!
All orange groves have golden gushings:
All mornings dawn with golden flushings!
In a shower of gold, say fables old,
A maiden was won by the god of gold. . . .

" . . . Lo, a vision . . . A vast and silent
bay, belted by silent villages . . . a thou-

sand paths, marked with footprints, all inland leading, none village-ward; and strown
with traces, as of a flying host. On: over
forest—hill, and dale—and lo! the golden
region! After the glittering spoil, by
strange river-margins, and beneath impend-
ing cliffs, thousands delve in quicksands; and,
sudden, sink in graves of their own making:
with gold dust mingling their own ashes.
. . .

"With many camels, a sleek stranger
comes—pauses before the shining heaps, and
shows *his* treasures: yams and bread-fruit.
'Give, give,' the famished hunters cry—'a
thousand shekels for a yam!—a prince's ran-
som for a meal!' . . . Then he who toiled
not, dug not, slaved not, straight loads his
caravans with gold; regains the beach, and
swift embarks for home. 'Home, home!'
the hunters cry, with bursting eyes. 'With
this bright gold, could we but join our wait-
ing wives, who wring their hands on distant
shores, all then were well. But we can not
fly; our prows lie rotting on the beach. Ah!
home! thou only happiness!—better thy silver earnings than all these golden findings.
Oh, bitter end to all our hopes—we die in
golden graves.' "

From beginning to end, *Mardi* is gloriously

insane. One persists in the belief that Melville enjoyed every line of it, even in his most abstruse passages. In the midst of much superlative praise the book was, of course, viciously attacked. *Blackwood's Magazine* was sadly disgusted "on a perusal of a rubbishing rhapsody entitled Mardi." The *Dublin University Magazine* found it "one of the saddest, most melancholy, most deplorable and humiliating perversions of genius" in the language.

What was the effect of such criticism on Melville, the first directed primarily at his writing, is very clearly shown in the following letter, the first portion of which appears elsewhere in this volume under *Redburn.* It is a peculiarly significant and pathetic Melville document, sensitive and disillusioned, written from London, on December 14, 1849, while he was seeking to dispose of the manuscript of *White-Jacket,* and secure some advance from his London publisher with which to pay his pressing debts.

Speaking of a writer in need of money, Melville says:

" . . . and when he attempts anything higher, God help him and save him! for it is not with a hollow purse as with a hollow baloon—for a hollow purse makes the poet *sink*—witness 'Mardi.' . . .

"What a madness and anguish it is, that

an author can never—under no conceivable circumstances—be at all frank with his readers. Could I, for one, be frank with them, how would they cease their railing—those at least who have railed.

"In a little notice of the 'Oregon Trail' I once said something 'critical' about another man's book—I shall never do it again. Hereafter I shall no more stab at a book (in print, I mean) than I would stab at a man. I am but a poor mortal, and I admit that I learn by experience and not by divine intuition. Had I not written and published 'Mardi' in all likelihood I would not be as wise as I am now, or may be. For that thing was stabbed *at* (I do not say *through*) and therefore I am the wiser for it. . . .

H. Melville."

This is a very humble Melville, although there is a fine lift of the chin in that " . . . I do not say *through*." In the next letter, February 2, 1850, he is back again with his old ironical pen. The letter, incidentally, is a not unworthy sample of what is rapidly becoming a lost art:

"My dear Duyckinck—Tho' somewhat unusual for a donor I must beg to apologise for making you the accompanying present of 'Mardi.' But no one who knows your li-

brary can doubt that such a choice conserva-
tory of exotics and other rare things in literature, after being long enjoyed by yourself,
must to a late posterity be preserved intact
by your descendants. How natural then—
tho' vain—in your friend to desire a place in
it for a plant, which tho' now unblown (em-
blematically, the leaves, you perceive, are
uncut) may possibly—by some miracle, that
is—flower like the aloe, a hundred years
hence—or not flower at all, which is more
likely by far, for some aloes never flower.

"Again: (as the divines say) political re-
publics should be the asylum for the persecuted of all nations; so, if 'Mardi' be
admitted to your shelves, your bibliographi-
cal Republic of Letters may find some con-
tentment in the thought that it has afforded
refuge to a book which almost everywhere
else has been driven forth like a wild, mystic
Mormon into shelterless exile.

"The leaves, I repeat, are uncut—let them
remain so—and let me supplementarily hint
that a bit of old parchment (from some old
Arabic M.S.S. on Astrology) tied around
each volume, and sealed on the back with a
Sphynx and never to be broken till the aloe
flowers—would not be an unsuitable device
for the bookbinding of 'Mardi.'

"That book is a sort of dose, if you please,

tho' in the present case charitably administered in three parts instead of two. . . .

Truly yours,

H. Melville."

The reference in the last paragraph is to the
London three-volume edition, the American edition having been in two volumes. The letter,
written nearly a year after the publication of the
book, bears unmistakable evidence of its failure.
But the hundred years have nearly passed, perhaps the aloe will yet in time flower!

VI

REDBURN

IN June, 1837, when he was not quite eighteen, Melville shipped before the mast in New York, aboard of the *Highlander,* of which he says in *Redburn:*

" . . . you must know that the Highlander was not a Liverpool liner, or packet-ship, plying in connection with a sisterhood of packets, at stated intervals, between the two ports. No: she was only what is called a *regular trader* to Liverpool; sailing upon no fixed days, and acting very much as she pleased, being bound by no obligations of any kind; though in all her voyages, ever having New York or Liverpool for her destination. Merchant vessels which are neither liners nor regular traders, among sailors come under the general head of *transient ships,* which implies that they are here today, and somewhere else tomorrow, like Mullins's dog. . . .

"He [*the figurehead*] was a gallant six-footer of a Highlander 'in full fig,' with bright tartans, bare knees, barred leggings, and blue bonnet, and the most vermilion of cheeks. He was game to his wooden marrow, and stood up to it through thick and thin; one foot a little advanced, and his right arm stretched forward, daring on the waves. In a gale of wind it was glorious to watch him standing at his post like a hero, and plunging up and down the watery Highlands and Lowlands, as the ship went foaming on her way. . . ."

Melville himself went aboard with a gray shooting-jacket with "fine long skirts, stout horn buttons, and plenty of pockets," and the clothes which he had brought from home, including his "best pair of pantaloons . . . a very conspicuous and remarkable looking pair."

"I had had them made to order by our village tailor," he says. "Now this old tailor had shown me the pattern after which he intended to make my pantaloons; but I improved upon it, and bade him have a slit on the outside of each leg, at the foot, to button up with a row of six brass bell buttons; for a grown-up cousin of mine who was a great sportsman, used to wear a beautiful pair of pantaloons, made precisely in that way. . . .

"The sailors made a great deal of fun of

them . . . showing very plainly that they had no idea that my pantaloons were a very genteel pair, made in the height of the sporting fashion, and copied from my cousin's, who was a young man of fortune and drove a Tilbury."

He wore, moreover, his Sunday boots, which fitted him to a charm. They were, it seems:

" . . . a beautiful pair of boots. But all this only unfitted them the more for sea-service; as I soon discovered. They had very high heels, which were all the time tripping me in the rigging . . . and the salt water made them shrink in such a manner that they pinched me terribly about the instep. . . . The legs were quite long, coming a good way up towards my knees, and the edges were mounted with red morocco. The sailors used to call them my 'gaff-topsail-boots.' "

These articles Melville supplemented, to the extent of two dollars and forty-nine cents, with "a red woollen shirt near Catherine Market, a tarpaulin hat, which I got at an out-door stand near Peck Slip, a belt and a jack-knife, and two or three trifles." One of his last acts ashore was to try on the shirt, "to see what sort of a looking sailor I was going to make," after which he took a pair of scissors and "went to cutting my hair, which was very long." One would cheerfully give a complete first edition of Melville for a picture of him thus "in full fig," pantaloons, topboots and all!

On August 18, 1849, Melville published *Redburn,* in which he gives a detailed account of that voyage to Liverpool and back, and of his experiences in the forecastle, and among the "booble alleys" of Liverpool. The book is dedicated to his younger brother, Thomas Melville, "now a sailor on a voyage to China," who subsequently became captain of the clipper-ship *Meteor.*

Among the most striking features of the book are Melville's descriptions of his shipmates. The sinister Jackson, who—

" . . . was as yellow as gamboge, had no more whiskers on his cheek than I have on my elbows. His hair had fallen out, and left him very bald, except in the nape of his neck, and just behind the ears, where it was stuck over with short little tufts, and looked like a worn-out shoe brush. His nose had broken down in the middle, and he squinted with one eye, and did not look very straight out of the other. He dressed a good deal like a Bowery boy; for he despised the ordinary sailor rig; wearing a pair of great overall blue trousers, fastened with suspenders, and

three red woolen shirts, one over the other
. . . and he had a large white wool hat,
with a broad rolling brim. . . . He might
have seen thirty, or perhaps fifty years. . . .
Nothing was left of this Jackson but the foul
lees and dregs of a man; he was thin as a
shadow; nothing but skin and bones. . . ."

The black cook, Mr. Thompson, "a serious old
fellow, much given to metaphysics, and used to
talk about original sin." The steward, a handsome, dandy mulatto, who had once been a barber
in West Broadway and went by the name of
Lavender. He sported an uncommon head of
frizzled hair, which he kept—

" . . . well perfumed with Cologne water.
. . . His clothes, being mostly cast-off suits
of the Captain of a London liner . . . were
all in the height of the exploded fashions,
and of every kind of color and cut. He had
claret colored suits, and snuff colored suits,
and red velvet vests, and buff and brimstone
pantaloons. . . . He was a sentimental sort
of darky, and read the 'Three Spaniards,'
and 'Charlotte Temple,' and carried a lock
of frizzled hair in his vest pocket, which he
frequently volunteered to show to people,
with his handkerchief to his eyes."

[48]

The sailor, Max, with his lugubrious library consisting of an account of *Shipwrecks and Disasters
at Sea,* and a large black volume with *Delirium
Tremens* in great gilt letters on the back. And
Jack Blunt, "a curious looking fellow . . . and
a little given to looking at sea-life romantically"—

" . . . singing songs about susceptible mer-
maids who fell in love with handsome young
oyster boys and gallant fishermen. And he
had . . . another incomprehensible story
about a sort of fairy sea-queen who used to
be dunning a sea captain all the time for his
autograph to boil in some eel soup, for a spell
against the scurvy. . . .

"And he frequently related his interviews
in Liverpool with a fortune-teller, an old
negro woman by the name of De Squak . . .
and how she had two black cats, with re-
markably green eyes, and night caps on their
heads, solemnly seated on a claw-footed
table near the old goblin, when she felt his
pulse, to tell what was going to befall him."

This Blunt was a devotee of "Trafalgar Oil for
restoring the hair," supplemented by applications
of "Balm of Paradise, or the Elixir of the Battle
of Copenhaguen." He was also the possessor of
the *Bonaparte Dream Book,* purporting to be—

" . . . the self-same system by aid of which

Napoleon Bonaparte had risen in the world
from being a corporal to an emperor. . . .
Every morning before taking his pills and
applying his hair oils, he [*Blunt*] would steal
out of his bunk before the rest of the watch
were awake, take out his pamphlet and a bit
of chalk . . . and begin scratching his oily
head to remember his fugitive dreams. . . ."

Of *Redburn,* Mr. Masefield has said:

"The book I love best of his is one very
difficult to come by. . . . It is the romance
of his own boyhood. I mean *Redburn.* Any
number of good pens will praise the known
books . . . perhaps *Redburn* will have fewer
praises, so here goes for *Redburn,* a boy's
book about running away to sea. . . ."

It is interesting to turn back from this to that
letter of Melville's, the conclusion of which has
already been quoted in this volume under *Mardi.*
As explained in that section, the letter was written from abroad, in December, 1849, at a time
when Melville was in considerable financial
trouble.

He had sailed on October 11, 1849, from New
York aboard the packet *Southampton.* The
reference in the letter to the cutting off of his
"travelling tail," has to do with the abandoning

from lack of funds of a projected journey to Constantinople, Greece, and Egypt, which he was to have undertaken with two fellow passengers, Mr. Adler, a German scholar, and Mr. Taylor, a cousin of James Bayard Taylor. Owing to the confused state of the copyright question in England of which he complains, Melville found it necessary to remain in London for the purpose of placing the manuscript of *White-Jacket,* contenting himself with a flying trip to Paris, Brussels, Cologne, and Coblentz, which he made during the interval between the two dates given in the following letter—a letter which gives a graphic impression of the conditions under which *Redburn* was written, and of Melville's own estimate of that work:

"Paris, Dec. 2, 1849.

"My dear Mr. Duyckinck . . .

"The other evening I went to see Rachel —and having taken my place in the *'que'* (how the devil do you spell it?) or tail—and having waited there for full an hour—upon at last arriving at the ticket-box the woman then closed her little wicket in my face—and so the 'tail' was cut off.

"Now my travelling 'tail' has been cut off in like manner, by the confounded state of the copyright question in England. . . .

[51]

"London, Dec. 14, '49.

"My dear Duyckinck—I meant to send this to you by a Havre packet—but learning more about her did not. . . .

"I did not see your say about the book 'Redburn,' which to my surprise (somewhat) seems to have been favorably received. I am glad of it, for it puts money into an empty purse. But I hope I shall never write such a book again.

"Tho' when a poor devil writes with duns all around him, and looking over the back of his chair, and perching on his pen, and dancing in his ink-stand—like the devils about St. Anthony—what can you expect of that poor devil? What but a beggarly 'Redburn.'

"But we that write and print have all our books predestinated—and for me, I shall write such things as the Great Publisher of mankind ordained ages before he published The World. . . .

H. Melville."

VII

HAWTHORNE

IN 1850, Melville and Hawthorne both took up their residence in the Berkshires. Melville settled in the Pittsfield farm which he christened Arrowhead, Hawthorne at Lenox in, as he says, "the very ugliest little bit of an old red farmhouse you ever saw." Melville was thirty-one years old, Hawthorne fifteen years older. The two men became distant neighbors, and, one is supposed to believe, close friends.

Mr. Weaver, in his *Herman Melville, Mariner and Mystic,* quotes a number of letters from Melville to Hawthorne, in which one is tempted to remark that Melville ventures to treat Hawthorne as an equal.

"I should have a paper-mill established at one end of the house," he says once, "and so have an extra riband for foolscap rolling in upon my desk, and upon that endless riband I should write a thousand—a million—a billion thoughts, all under the form of a letter to you. The divine magnet is on you, and

my magnet responds. Which is the bigger?
A foolish question—they are *one*.

H."

Again in a postscript he says to Hawthorne
that:

"This 'all' feeling. . . . You must often
have felt it, lying on the grass on a warm
summer's day. Your legs seem to send out
shoots into the earth. Your hair feels like
leaves upon your head! This is the *all* feeling. . . . You must not fail to admire my
discretion in paying the postage on this letter."

It seems unlikely, however, that Hawthorne
ever experienced any such pagan sensations. In
another letter Melville presumes to suggest to
Hawthorne that:

" . . . I shall roll down to you, my good
fellow, seeing we—that is, you and I—must
hit upon some little bit of vagabondage before autumn comes. Greylock—we must go
and vagabondise there. . . ."

This to the man whose acquaintances "formed
but a tiny arc in the great circle of his compre-
hension," who "was worshipped, idolised, can-
onised." One can not rid oneself of the
impression that Melville was forever slapping

Hawthorne on the back, to the unaccustomed surprise and private displeasure of the latter. One suspects that the jocular Melville shared the error of those who—

" . . . seeing his [*Hawthorne's*] congenial aspect towards their little round of habits and beliefs . . . would leap to the conclusion that he was no more and no less than one of themselves. . . ."

In other words, one wonders, when all was said and done, whether Melville did not take a mile of Hawthorne's friendship for every inch vouchsafed.

It is interesting to turn from these speculations to the following letter, written by Melville in February, 1851, in which he voices his private impressions of his august neighbor, and suggests a salutary addition to his "plump sphericality":

Pittsfield, Wednesday, 1851.

"My dear Duyckinck . . . After a long procrastination I went down to see Mr. Hawthorne a couple of weeks ago. I found him, of course, buried in snow; and the delightful scenery about him all wrapped up and tucked away under a napkin as it were. He was to have made me a day's visit, and I had promised myself much pleasure in getting him up in my snug room here, and dis-

[55]

cussing the universe with a bottle of brandy and cigars. But he has not been able to come, owing to sickness in his family—or else he's up to the lips in the *Universe* again.

"By the way, I have recently read his 'Twice Told Tales' (I hadn't read but a few of them before). I think they far exceed the 'Mosses.' They are, I fancy, an earlier vintage from his vine. Some of those sketches are wonderfully subtle. Their deeper meanings are worthy of a Brahmin. Still there is something lacking—a good deal lacking to the plump sphericality of the man. What is that? He doesn't patronise the butcher—he needs roast-beef, done rare.

"Nevertheless, for one, I regard Hawthorne (in his books) as evincing a quality of genius immensely loftier, and more profound, too, than any other American has shown hitherto in the printed form. Irving is a grasshopper to him—putting the souls of the two men together, I mean. But I must close. . . .

Truly yours,

H. Melville."

VIII

ARROWHEAD

1850-1851

I

IN the fall of 1850 Melville installed himself in the farmhouse which he had purchased near Pittsfield, Massachusetts, on Holmes Road, and which he christened Arrowhead. In the *Piazza Tales*, published in 1856, Melville thus describes the house:

> "When I removed into the country it was to occupy an old-fashioned farm house . . . the country round about was such a picture. . . . The circle of the stars cut by the circle of the mountains. At least so it looks from the house, though once upon the mountains, no circle of them can you see. Had the site been chosen five rods off this charmed circle would not have been.
> "The house is old. Seventy years since, from the heart of the Hearth Stone Hill, they quarried the Kaaba or Holy Stone, to which, each Thanksgiving, the social pilgrim

used to come. So long ago that in digging for the foundation, the workmen used both spade and axe fighting the Troglodytes of those subterranean parts—sturdy roots of a sturdy wood, encamped upon what is now a long landslide of sleeping meadow, sloping away from my poppy bed. Of that knit wood, but one survivor stands—an elm, lonely through steadfastness.

"Whoever built the house, he builded better than he knew, or else Orion in the zenith flashed down his Damocles' sword to him some starry night and said 'Build there.' For how, otherwise, could it have entered the builder's mind that, upon the clearing being made, such a purple prospect would be his? Nothing less than Greylock, with all his hills about him, like Charlemagne among his peers. . . ."

Upon this house, for the sake of Greylock, Melville built a piazza to the north, of which he says:

"But, even in December, this Northern piazza does not repel—nipping cold and gusty though it be, and the North wind, like any miller, bolting by the snow in finest flour —for then, once more, with frosted beard, I pace the sleety deck, weathering Cape Horn.

"In Summer, too, Canute-like, sitting here,
one is often reminded of the sea. For not
only do long ground-swells roll the slant-
ing grain, and little wavelets of the grass rip-
ple over upon the low piazza, as their beach,
and the blown down of dandelions is wafted
like the spray, and the purple of the moun-
tains is just the purple of the billows, and a
still August noon broods over the deep
meadows, as a calm upon the Line; but the
vastness and the lonesomeness are so oceanic,
and the silence and the sameness, too, that
the first peep of a strange house, rising beyond the trees, is for all the world like
spying, on the Barbary coast, an unknown
sail."

The house was built in 1780 by Captain David
Bush, and has a chimney twelve feet square, so
one learns in Mr. Weaver's *Herman Melville;*
the old kitchen fireplace being large enough to
accommodate a four-foot log. Of this chimney
Melville wrote in *I and My Chimney, (Putnam's
Monthly Magazine,* March, 1856):

" . . . here I keep mysterious cordials of a
choice, mysterious flavor, made so by the
constant maturing and subtle ripening of the
chimney's gentle heat, distilled through that
warm mass of masonry. Better for wines it

[59]

is than voyages to the Indies; my chimney itself is a tropic. A chair by my chimney in a November day is as good for an invalid as a long season spent in Cuba. Often I think how grapes might ripen against my chimney. How my wife's geraniums bud there! But in December. Her eggs too—can't keep them near the chimney on account of hatching. Ah, a warm heart has my chimney. . . ."

In Mr. Weaver's book, again, one finds a quotation from the Pittsfield reminiscences of Colonel Richard Lathers, who was one of Melville's nearest neighbors, and who gives this pleasant picture of Arrowhead:

"I visited him often in his well-stocked library, where I listened with intense pleasure to his highly individual views of society and politics. He always provided a bountiful supply of good cider—the product of his own orchard—and of tobacco, in the virtues of which he was a firm believer. Indeed, he prided himself on the inscription painted over his capacious fire-place: 'I and my chimney smoke together,' an inscription I have seen strikingly verified more than once when the atmosphere was heavy and the wind was east."

In this house, and in this environment, Melville wrote *Moby-Dick* and *Pierre*.

Moby-Dick, undoubtedly Melville's masterpiece—the book of which Mr. Masefield says that "in that wild, beautiful romance Melville seems to have spoken the very secret of the sea, and to have drawn into his tale all the magic, all the sadness, all the wild joy of many waters. It stands quite alone; quite unlike any other book known to me. It strikes a note which no other sea writer has ever struck"—was written in 1850-1851, and published in 1851.

The book is a compendium of all of Melville's literary tendencies. It contains allegory, natural history, philosophy, rhapsody, oratory, character study, and humor. It presents one of the most vivid and detailed studies of the whale and of its capture in the language; of—

> " . . . all the Leviathans of note," and also "a rabble of uncertain, fugitive, half-fabulous whales. . . . The Bottle-Nose Whale; the Junk Whale; the Pudding-Headed Whale; the Cape Whale; the Leading Whale; the Cannon Whale; the Scragg Whale; the Coppered Whale; the Elephant Whale; the Iceberg Whale; the Quog Whale; the Blue Whale. . . ."

It concerns itself with "the fiery hunt" for

Moby-Dick, the Great White Whale, of whom Melville says that:

" . . . it was not so much his uncommon bulk that so much distinguished him from other sperm whales, but . . . a peculiar, snow-white wrinkled forehead, and a high, pyramidical white hump. These were his prominent features; the tokens whereby, even in the limitless, uncharted seas, he revealed his identity, at a long distance, to those who knew him.

"The rest of his body was so streaked, and spotted, and marbled with the same shrouded hue, that, in the end, he had gained his distinctive appellation of the White Whale; a name, indeed, literally justified by his vivid aspect, when seen gliding at high noon through a dark blue sea, leaving a milky-way wake of creamy foam, all spangled with golden gleamings.

"Nor was it his unwonted magnitude, nor his remarkable hue, nor yet his deformed lower jaw, that so much invested the whale with natural terror, as that unexampled, intelligent malignity which . . . he had over and over again evinced in his assaults. More than all, his treacherous retreats struck more of dismay than perhaps aught else. For, when swimming before his exulting pursuers, with every apparent symptom of alarm, he had several times been known to turn round suddenly, and, bearing down upon them, either stave their boats to splinters, or drive them back in consternation to their ship. . . . Such seemed the White Whale's infernal aforethought of ferocity, that every dismembering or death that he caused was not wholly regarded as having been inflicted by an unintelligent agent. . . ."

It concludes with the three-day conflict between Moby-Dick and the crew of the *Pequod,* during which—

"Suddenly the waters around them slowly swelled in broad circles; then quickly upheaved, as if sideways sliding from a submerged berg of ice, swiftly rising to the surface. A low rumbling sound was heard, a subterraneous hum; and then all held their breaths; as bedraggled with trailing ropes, and harpoons, and lances, a vast form shot lengthwise, but obliquely from the sea. Shrouded in a thin drooping veil of mist, it hovered for a moment in the rainbowed air; and then fell swamping back into the deep. Crushed thirty feet upwards, the waters flashed for an instant like heaps of fountains, then brokenly sank in a shower of flakes, leaving the circling surface creamed

like new milk round the marble trunk of
the whale. . . ."

until finally—

"From the ship's bows, nearly all the seamen now hung inactive . . . all their enchanted eyes intent upon the whale, which
from side to side strangely vibrating his pre-
destinating head, sent a broad band of over-
spreading semicircular foam before him as
he rushed.   Retribution, swift vengeance,
eternal malice were in his whole aspect, and
spite of all that man could do, the solid white
buttress of his forehead smote the ship's
starboard bow, till men and timbers reeled.
. . . Through the breach, they heard the
waters pour, as mountain torrents down a
flume. . . ."

This disaster was based on the actual fate
which overtook the whaler *Essex,* out of Nan-
tucket, in 1819.

These extracts may serve to give a glimpse of
the scope and nature of this gigantic work, which
The Literary World described as "an intellectual
chowder of romance, philosophy, natural history,
fine writing, bad sayings;" and of which the *Dublin University Magazine* said that "it is quite as
eccentric and monstrously extravagant in many of
its incidents as even *Mardi.* . . ."

Pierre was written during the summer of 1851, and published in 1852. The book contains much autobiographical material concerning Melville's childhood, and then develops into a sinister story of incest, murder, and suicide. Mr. Weaver says that "in *Pierre,* Melville coiled down into the night of his soul, to write an anatomy of despair." The London *Men of the Time* condemned it as "an unhealthy, mystic romance;" *The Literary World,* edited by the friendly Duyckinck, found nothing better to say of it than that it must be received "as an eccentricity of the imagination. The most unmoral *moral* of the story, if it has any moral at all, seems to be the impracticability of virtue. . . . It is alone intelligible as an unintelligibility."

The book was of course a disastrous failure; it brought forth a more vicious hurricane of abuse than had ever before been directed against Melville; it has in many quarters been set down as the chief reason for the almost total extinction, subsequently, of Melville's light in the world of letters.

2

And yet at the very time when his mind must have been full of the thoughts and moods which found expression in *Moby-Dick,* and, more particularly, in *Pierre,* Melville was writing the simple, charming, humorous, impulsive letters which

[65]

follow. And those few, patient paragraphs, from which one learns of his infirmity—not that "infirmity of jocularity" to which he refers once elsewhere, but the infirmity of failing eyesight.

The first of these letters it not written actually from Arrowhead, but from Broadhall, the old home of his uncle, Major Thomas Melville, to which the latter had brought his French wife, Françoise Raymonde Eulogie Marie des Douleurs Lamé Fleury, and where he resided with his second wife, Mary Anna Augusta Hobard, until his departure, in 1837, for Galena, Illinois. Melville, as a boy, had often visited his uncle Thomas in the house which, at the time this letter was written, had been converted into a hotel.

"Banian Hall, August 16, 1850.

"I call it Banian Hall, my dear Duyckinck, because it seems the old original Hall of this neighborhood—besides, it is a wide-spreading house, and the various outhouses seem shoots from it, that have taken root all round.

"I write you this from the *garret-way*, located at that little embrasure of a window (you must remember it) which commands so noble a view of Saddleback. My desk is an old one, an old thing of my uncle the Major's, which for twelve years back has been packed away in the corn-loft over the carriage house. Upon dragging it out to daylight, I found that it was covered with the marks of fowls—quite white with them —eggs had been laid in it—think of that! Is it not typical of those other eggs that authors may be said to lay in their desks, especially those with pigeon-holes?

"Day before yesterday—Wednesday—I received your letter of the 13th, also Mathews', and was delighted and softened by both. . . .

"Twelve more beautiful babies than you sent me in that wicker cradle by Express I have never seen. Uncommon intelligence was in their aspect, and they seem full of animation and hilarity. I have no doubt, if they were let alone a while, they would all grow to be demijohns. In a word, my dear Fellow, they were but too well thought of you, because so much more than I deserved.

"Let me now tell you how that precious basket was carried in state to the farm, something like the Flitch of bacon. A gentleman and a lady arrived here as boarders yesterday morning. In the afternoon in four carriages a party of us went to Lebanon. Returning, we stopped at the Express office in the village; and then, with the basket borne before me at my feet, I drove off full speed followed by the whole galloping pro-

[67]

cession. Today, at dinner, we cracked the champagne, and our full glass (all around the table) was Mr. Duyckinck and Mr. Mathews.

"But the cigars! The Oriental looking box! and the Antilles smell of them! And the four different thrones and denominations of bundles, all harmonizing together like the Iroquois. Had there been two more bundles I should have called them the Six Nations. . . .

"If it is a fair day I shall drive to Hawthorne's tomorrow and deliver his parcels.
. . .

Goodbye

H. Melville."

There is something generous about the broad generality of the date of the next, and subsequent, letters.

"Sunday evening 1850.

"My dear Duyckinck . . . It has been a most glowing and Byzantine day—the heavens reflecting the hues of the October apples in the orchard—nay, the heavens themselves looking so ripe and ruddy, that it must be harvest-home with the angels, and Charles' Wain be heaped high as Saddleback with Autumn's sheaves. You should see the

maples—you should see the young perennial
pines—the red blazings of the one contrast-
ing with the painted green of the others, and
the wide flushings of the autumn an harmonizing [——]. I tell you that sunrises and
sunsets grow side by side in these woods, and
momentarily moult in the falling leaves. . . .

Truly yours

H. Melville."

The next letter, received on December 12,
1850, contains the first reference to Melville's
eyes. The original letter, while a very long one,
is literally scrawled unevenly across the paper,
misspelled, and in parts almost illegible. It is,
however, an invaluable document of the conditions under which *Moby-Dick* was written.

Friday evening
Pittsfield.

"My dear Duyckinck . . . Before I go
further let me say here that I am writing
this by candle light—an uncommon thing
with me—and therefore my writing won't be
very legible, because I am keeping one eye
shut and wink at the paper with the other.

"If you expect a letter from a man who
lives in the country you must make up your
mind to receive an egotistical one—for he

[69]

has no gossip nor news of any kind, unless the neighbor's cow has calved or the hen laid a silver egg. . . .

"I have a sort of sea-feeling here in the country, now that the ground is all covered with snow. I look out of my window in the morning when I rise as I would out of a port-hole of a ship in the Atlantic. My room seems a ship's cabin; and at nights when I wake up and hear the wind shrieking, I almost fancy there is too much sail on the house, and I had better go on the roof and rig in the chimney.

"Do you want to know how I pass my time? I rise at eight—thereabouts—and go to my barn—say good morning to the horse and give him his breakfast. (It goes to my heart to give him a cold one, but it can't be helped.) Then, pay a visit to my cow—cut up a pumpkin or two for her, and stand by to see her eat it—for it's a pleasant sight to see a cow move her jaws—she does it so mildly and with such a sanctity.

"My own breakfast over, I go to my work-room and light my fire—then spread my M.S.S. on the table—take one business squint at it, and fall to with a will. At 2-1/2 P. M. I hear a preconcerted knock at my door, which (by request) continues till I rise and go to the door, which seems to wean me ef-

fectively from my writing, however interested
I may be.

"My friends the horse and cow then de-
mand their dinner—and I go and give it
them. My own dinner over, I rig my sleigh
and with my mittens and rubbers start off for
the village—and if it be a 'Literary World'
day, great is the satisfaction thereof.

"My evenings I spend in a sort of mes-
meric state in my room—not being able to
read—only now and then skimming over
some large-printed book.

"Can you send me about fifty fast-writing
youths, with an easy style and not averse to
polishing their letters(?). If you can I wish
you would, because since I have been here I
have planned about that number of future
works and can't find enough time to think
about them separately.

"But I don't know but a book in a man's
brain is better off than a book bound in calf
—at any rate it is safer from criticism. And
taking a book off the brain, is akin to the
ticklish and dangerous business of taking an
old painting off a panel—you have to scrape
off the whole brain in order to get at it with
due safety—and even then the painting may
not be worth the trouble. . . .

H. Melville."

In the next letter, received on February 14, 1851, Melville takes a spirited flier at publicity.

"Pittsfield, Wednesday, 1851.
"My dear Duyckinck

" 'A dash of salt spray'!—Where am I to get salt spray here in inland Pittsfield? I shall have to import it from foreign parts. All I now have to do with salt is when I salt my horse and cow—not *salt them down,* I don't mean that (tho' indeed I have before now dined on 'salt-horse') but when I give them their weekly salt, by way of seasoning all their week's meals in one prospective lump.

"How shall a man go about refusing a man? Best be roundabout, or plump on the mark?—I can not write the thing you want. I am in the humor to lend a hand to a friend if I can; but I am not in the humor to write the kind of thing you need—and I am not in the humor to write for Holden's Magazine. If I were to go on to give you all my reasons you would pronounce me a bore so I will not do that. You must be content to believe that I *have* reasons, or else I would not refuse so small a thing.

"As for the Daguerriotype (I spell the word right from your sheet) that's what I can not send you, because I have none. And if I had, I would not send it for such a purpose, even to you—Pshaw! you cry—and so cry I.—'This is intensified vanity, not true modesty or anything of that sort!'—Again I say so too.   But if it be so, how can I help it.   The fact is, almost everybody is having his 'mug' engraved nowadays, so that this test of distinction is getting to be reversed; and therefore, to see one's 'mug' in a magazine, is presumptive evidence that he's a nobody.   So being as vain a man as ever lived, and feeling that my illustrious name is famous throughout the world—I respectfully decline being *oblivionated* by a Dagreutype (what a devil of an unspellable word!). . . .

Truly yours

H. Melville."

The next brief extract contains the most significant paragraph in the entire series.

"Pittsfield, Wednesday, 1851

"My dear Duyckinck . . . The spring begins to open upon Pittsfield but slowly.   I only wish that I had more day-time to spend out *in the day;* but like an owl I steal about by twilight, owing to the twilight of my eyes. . . .

H. Melville."

In the next letter, received on November 9, 1851, Melville refers to the disaster to the whale-ship *Ann Alexander,* of New Bedford, rammed and sunk by a whale on August 20, 1851, and a full account of which appeared in *The Literary World.* The allusion to Norman de Wardt is probably in connection with an incident of whale fishery with which Melville was not familiar during the writing of *Moby-Dick.*

"Pittsfield, Friday afternoon.

"Dear Duyckinck—Your letter received last night had a sort of stunning effect on me. For some days past being engaged in the woods with axe, wedge, and [———], the Whale had almost completely slipped me for the time (and I was the merrier for it) when Crash! comes Moby-Dick himself (as you justly say) and reminds me of what I have been about for part of the last year or two. It is really and truly a surprising coincidence, to say the least. I make no doubt it *is* Moby-Dick himself, for there is no account of his capture after the sad fate of the Pequod about fourteen years ago—

"Ye Gods! What a Commentator is this Ann Alexander whale. What he has to say is short and pithy but very much to the point. I wonder if my evil art has raised this monster.

[74]

"The Behring Strait disaster too, and the cording (?) along the New Foundland coast of those scores and scores of fishermen, and the inland gales on the Lakes. Verily the pot boileth inside and out. And woe unto us, we but live in the days that have been. Yet even then they found time to be jolly.

"Why didn't you send me that inestimable item of 'Norman de Wardt' before? Oh, had I but had that pie to cut into! But that and many other fine things doubtless are omitted. All one can do is to pick up what chip he can lying round him. They have no Vatican (as you have) in Pittsfield here. . . .

"For us here, winter is coming. The hills and the noses begin to look blue, and the trees have stripped themselves for the December tussle. I have had my dressing gown patched up, and got some wood in the woodhouse, and—by the way—have in full blast our great dining-room fireplace, which swallows down cords of wood as a whale does boats. . . .

H. Melville."

Aside from the intimate glimpses of Melville afforded by these letters, the most significant feature of them is the repeated reference to his failing eyesight. He is obliged to shut one eye and wink with the other when, in a rare instance, he writes by candlelight. He can not read in the evening, except occasionally to skim over a large-printed book. Owl-like, he must steal about in the twilight.

In August, 1851, Melville was thirty-two. He had, up to that time—that is, since 1846—written seven books. From 1851 until his death in 1891 he wrote only eight more, four of which were volumes of verse, and one of which remains unpublished. His first published book after *Pierre* in 1852 was *Israel Potter* in 1855. From the completion of *Pierre* in 1851 until the writing of *Israel Potter,* some time in 1854, with the exception of a few magazine articles, Melville apparently wrote nothing.

In December, 1850, he complained that he had not enough time to devote to the "fifty" works which he had in mind. Is the adverse criticism heaped upon *Pierre* the real cause of his silence during the next few years?

Or had the twilight of his eyes deepened?

The eyes which Mrs. Hawthorne objected to because they were neither large nor deep. Not keen eyes, either, and quite undistinguished. The eyes that sometimes had an indrawn, dim look.
. . .

Tired eyes?

IX

AN UNPUBLISHED MANUSCRIPT

IN 1859, so one learns from Mr. Weaver's *Herman Melville*, Mrs. Melville wrote to her mother, Mrs. Lemuel Shaw, that—

"Herman has taken to writing poetry. You need not tell anyone, for you know how such things get around."

This statement obviously refers to the manuscript mentioned in the letters reproduced below. That it was not made in a disparaging sense is evident from the correspondence.

As to the manuscript itself, since it can not be that of *Battle-Pieces*, published in 1866, the contents of which deal with the Civil War, it is more than likely that it is that of *Clarel*, finally published in 1876, at the expense of Melville's uncle. This seems all the more probable when one takes into consideration the fact that *Clarel* is the result of Melville's voyage to the Holy Land in 1856, and that the present manuscript was apparently written during the years immediately following his return.

In the first two letters reference is made to Melville's brother Allan, and to his proposed voyage around the Horn aboard the clipper *Meteor*, commanded by his younger brother, Thomas. The *Meteor*, a vessel of 1063 tons, was built in 1852 by Briggs Brothers, of South Boston, and owned by Curtis and Peabody, of Boston. Her record trip was in 1855, Boston to San Francisco in 108 days. In the second letter Melville speaks of proceeding to Manila, but he actually left the *Meteor* in San Francisco and returned in October aboard the *Carter* to Panama, and thence aboard the *North Star* to New York.

"Pittsfield, May 21st, 1860.

"Dear Duyckinck: If you have met Allan lately he has perhaps informed you that in a few days I go with my brother Tom a voyage round Cape Horn. It was only determined upon a short time since; and I am at present busy, as you may imagine, in getting ready for a somewhat long absence, and likewise in preparing for type certain M.S.S.

"Now may I with propriety ask of you, conditionally, a favor? Will you, upon the arrival of the M.S.S. in New York—that is, in the course of two weeks, or less—look over them and if they seem of a sort that you care to be any way concerned with, advise with Allan as to a publisher, and form of

[78]

volume, etc. And, since I can hardly summon the impudence to ask you in the midst of better avocations, to go over the proof-sheets; and there appears to be no one, in fact, to attend to that matter but the printer —will you at least see that the printer's proof reader is a careful and competent hand?—

"In short, may I, without seeming too confident, ask you, as a veteran and expert in these matters, and as an old acquaintance, to lend something of an overseeing eye to the launching of this craft—the committing of it to the elements?

"Remember me with kindest regards to your brother, and answer me as soon as you can; and whether you say yea or nay, Believe me,

Sincerely yours,
H. Melville."

"Boston, May 29th, 1860.
On board ship 'Meteor'

"My dear Duyckinck: I am glad that the postponement of the ship's day of sailing gives me a chance to answer your letter, received, in reply to mine, on the eve of my leaving Pittsfield. It was a very welcome one—quite a wind from the fields of old times.

"My wife will send you the parcel in the course of a week or so—there remaining something to be finished in copying the M.S.S.

"As my wife has interested herself a good deal in this matter, and in fact seems to know more about it than I do—at least about the *merits* of the performance—I must therefore refer you to her, in case of any exigency requiring information further than you are now in possession of.

"If your brother George is not better employed, I hope he will associate himself with you in looking over my scribblings.

"That is enough in the egotistic way. Now for something else.

"I anticipate as much pleasure as, at the age of forty, one temperately can, on the voyage I am going. I go under very happy auspices so far as ship and captain is concerned. A noble ship and a nobler captain—and he my brother. We have the breadth of those tropics before us, to sail over twice, and shall round the world. Our first port is San Francisco, which we shall probably make in 110 days from Boston. Thence we go to Manila—and thence, I hardly know where —I wish devoutly you were going along. I think it would agree with you. The prime requisite for enjoyment on sea voyages, for passengers, is 1st health—2nd good-nature. Both first-rate things, but not universally to be found.—At sea a fellow comes out. Salt water is like wine, in that respect.

"I have a good lot of books with me— such as they are—plenty of old periodicals— lazy reading for lazy latitudes—

"Here I am called away, and must close.
Goodbye to you
and God bless you.

H. Melville."

The next three letters, written after Melville had sailed, are from Mrs. Melville—Elizabeth Shaw, the daughter of Lemuel Shaw of Boston, one-time Chief Justice of the Commonwealth of Massachusetts, whom Melville married in 1847.

"Pittsfield, June 1, 1860.
"Mr. Duycinck,
My dear Sir,—
"On Monday or Tuesday of next week I shall forward to you by Express, the manuscript of which Herman wrote you, and with this I enclose a copy of the memoranda which he jotted down for Allan, according to his request.

"To this also should have been added an item which Herman omitted in his haste, and that is, that the book should be plainly bound

[81]

—that is, not over-gilt, and to 'blue and gold' I know he has a decided aversion. He may have mentioned it in his letters to you from Boston. . . .

Yours etc.,

E. S. Melville."

Mrs. Melville does not ever seem to have mastered the correct spelling of Mr. Duyckinck's name. As to Melville's taste in binding, it is an irony that his *Battle-Pieces* should have been bound in an atrocious shade of blue, lettered in gold!

Mrs. Melville's copy of the memoranda to Allan, dated May 22, 1860, is given below. In them Melville does not seem to have had any doubts concerning the publication of the manuscript.

"Memoranda for Allan

Concerning the publication of my verses.

"1. Don't stand on terms much with the publisher—half-profits after expenses are paid will content me—not that I expect much profits—but that will be a fair nominal arrangement. They should also give me 1 doz. copies of the book.

"2. Don't have the Harpers. I should like

the Appletons or Scribner. But Duycinck's advice will be good here.

"3. The sooner the thing is printed and published the better. The 'season' will make little or no difference, I fancy, in this case.

"4. After printing don't let the book hang back—but publish and have done.

"5. For God's sake don't have By the Author of 'Typee,' 'Piddledee,' etc., on the title-page.

"6. Let the title-page be simply

Poems

by

Herman Melville.

"7. Don't have any clap-trap announcements—and 'sensation' puffs—nor any extracts published previous to publication of the book. Have a decent publisher, in short.

"8. Don't take any measures, or make inquiries as to expediency of an English edition simultaneous with the American—as in case of 'Confidence Man.'

"9. In the M.S.S. each piece is on a page by itself, however small the piece. This was done merely for convenience in the final classification, and should be no guide for the printer. Of course in printing two or more pieces will sometimes appear on the same page—according to length of pieces etc. You understand.

"10. The poems are divided into books as you will see, but the divisions are not *called* books—they are only numbered. Thus it is in the M.S.S. and should be the same in print. There should be a page with the number between every division.

"11. Anything not perfectly plain in the M.S.S. can be referred to Lizzie, also have the M.S.S. returned to her after printing.

"12. Lizzie should by all means see the printed sheets *before* being bound, in order to detect any gross errors consequent upon misconstruing the M.S.S.

"These are the thoughts which hurriedly occur to me at this moment. Pardon the abruptness of their expression but time is precious—of all human events, perhaps the publication of a first volume of verses is the most insignificant; but though a matter of no moment to the world, it is still of some concern to the author—as these *Mem.* show. Pray, therefore, don't laugh at my *Mem.* but give heed to them, and so oblige

Your brother

Herman."

The hint of dissatisfaction with Harpers in this list of Melville "Don'ts" is interesting. And yet it was Harpers who published *Battle-Pieces* in 1866. To be sure the title-page of that book does not say By the Author of "Typee," "Piddledee," etc.!

The last two letters from Mrs. Melville complete the story of the unpublished manuscript.

                "Pittsfield, June 4th, 1860.
"Mr. Duycinck,
    My dear Sir,
    "I send you the manuscript and hope the printers will find no difficulty in reading it, though it has been (the greater part of it) necessarily copied in much haste. If anything in it should be obscure, please enclose the page to me and I will compare it with the original draught.

    "In making up the table of 'contents,' I am not sure that I have always used capitals in the right place. Will you have the kindness to overlook it, and right it, if wrong.

    "In the printed book, the titles of the verses are all in capitals, I believe, so of course the printer will arrange that, and I see that in the manuscript they are sometimes underscored which is accidental.

    "One question more occurs to me about titles, which is this—When the first line is quoted at the heading (as on page 111) what punctuation should be used about it?

Quotation marks and *period,* or with whatever punctuation immediately follows in the verse? With this the contents should also correspond.

"I am sorry to trouble you about these little matters, Mr. Duycinck, but Herman was obliged to leave much in an unfinished state, and I should feel much easier, as I know he would, if you would overlook the sheets for these little inaccuracies.

"When you have read the manuscript I should be very glad to have your opinion of it, as a whole, and you need not be afraid to say *exactly* what you think—I am the more desirous of this, because as yet, no one has seen the sheets, excepting two of Herman's sisters, who are now with me—and I want to know how they would strike an unprejudiced person. If your brother also would add his impressions, so much the better. . . .

Yours etc.

E. S. Melville."

"Arrowhead, June 23d. 1860.
"My dear Mr. Duycinck,
"I received yours of the 19th yesterday, and hasten to thank you for your kind endeavors about the manuscript, regretting that its course does not run smoothly thus

far. For myself, I am willing to wait patiently for the result, so that the publication is eventually accomplished—and do not consider its rejection by the publishers as any test of its merit in a literary point of view—well knowing, as Herman does also, that *poetry* is a comparatively uncalled for article in the public market.

"I suppose that if John Milton were to offer 'Paradise Lost' to the Harpers tomorrow, it would be promptly rejected as 'unsuitable,' not to say denounced as dull.

"I think infinitely more of yours and your brother's opinion of it, and feel more confidence in its worth, since it has been looked at by persons of judgment and taste than ever before—it has been such a profound secret between Herman and myself for so long that I rejoice to have my own prejudice in its favor confirmed by someone in whose appreciation we can feel confidence—for I do not believe you would speak favorably of it, unless you could do so sincerely, so for that your letter gives me great satisfaction.

"The name of one publishing firm in New York occurs to me who might possibly take a personal interest in the matter—that of 'Derby and Jackson' the first named being a brother-in-law of 'Toby' of Typee memory, if he is the same that I think he is, 'C. L.

Derby,' former 'Actuary of Cosmopolitan Art Association'—I do not know of what standing the firm may be, but I merely offer the hint, in case 'Rudd and Carleton' should decline to publish.

"I feel that you and Allan will do everything that is suitable and proper about it and am deeply sensible of your kindly efforts to further its success—indeed I feel that it is in better hands than even with Herman's own management for he might be disheartened at the outset by its rejection and perhaps withold it altogether, which would be a great disappointment to me.

"I am prepared to be very patient in any delay that may ensue, even when the book shall have been accepted for publication— bearing in mind the 'midsummer stagnation of trade'—'season'—and all that—though I shall count on your promised report of progress in good time. . . .

Yours truly,
E. S. Melville."

Melville himself, referring to his poetry, says the following, in a letter to his brother Thomas (the sea captain with whom he made the voyage in 1860), quoted by Mr. Weaver:

"Pittsfield, May 25th, 1862.

"My dear boy: (or, if that appears disrespectful)

My dear Captain: . . .

" . . . Since I have quoted poetry above, it puts me in mind of my own doggerel. You will be pleased to learn that I have disposed of a lot of it at a great bargain. In fact, a trunk-maker took the whole lot off my hands at ten cents the pound. So, when you buy a new trunk again, just peep at the lining and perhaps you may be rewarded by some glorious stanza staring you in the face and claiming admiration. If you were not such a devil of a ways off, I would send you a trunk, by way of presentation-copy.

"I can't help thinking what a luckless chap you were that voyage you had a poetaster with you. You remember the romantic moonlight night, when the conceited donkey repeated to you about three cables' length of his verses. But you bore it like a hero. I can't in fact recall one single *wince*. To be sure, you went to bed immediately upon the conclusion of the entertainment; but this much I am sure of, whatever were your sufferings, you never gave them utterance. . . .

Always your affectionate brother,

Herman."

This characteristic sample of what Melville calls elsewhere his "infirmity of jocularity" is evidently a reference to himself during the San Francisco voyage, and to the verses contained in the manuscript which he had just completed at that time.

* * * * *

In closing this series of Melville letters it is not thought out of place to reproduce some extracts from his verse, taken from "The Stone Fleet, an old sailor's lament, December, 1861," published in *Battle-Pieces*. The poem refers to the sinking of a fleet of old whalers loaded with stone at the entrance to Charleston harbor during the Civil War.

"I have a feeling for those ships,
  Each worn and ancient one,
  With great bluff bows, and broad in the
      beam:
  Ay, it was unkindly done.
      But so they serve the Obsolete—
      Even so, Stone Fleet!

"You'll say I'm doting; do but think
  I scudded round the Horn in one—
  The Tenedos, a glorious
  Good old craft as ever run—
      Sunk (how all unmeet!)
      With the Old Stone Fleet.

[90]

"An India ship of fame was she,
Spices and shawls and fans she bore;
A whaler when her wrinkles came—
Turned off! till, spent and poor,
        Her bones were sold (escheat)!
        Ah! Stone Fleet.

*   *   *   *   *

"To scuttle them—a pirate deed—
Sack them, and dismast;
They sunk so slow, they died so hard,
But gurgling dropped at last.
        Their ghosts in gales repeat
        Woe's us, Stone Fleet!"

*   *   *   *   *

PART II

BIBLIOGRAPHY

INTRODUCTION

M ANY lives, many bibliographies, of Melville will be written.

The present Bibliography is but a small effort towards a wider acquaintance with Melville's books. It presents no claims to completeness, no pretensions of infallibility. It is merely a preliminary statement intended to invite, if not call down, a fuller discussion. If, by reason of its very deficiencies, it succeeds in stimulating a more active research, it will largely have accomplished its purpose.

Besides magazine articles, book reviews, and other fugitive writings, fourteen books constitute the sum of Melville's published work. Of these, seven were published between the years 1846 and 1853, seven between the years 1853 and 1891. Melville was twenty-six when his first, seventy-two when his last, books were published. At the time of his death he had just completed another novel, *Billy Budd*, which remains unpublished, along with an accumulation of verse.

During the first period of seven years, Melville published *Typee*, in 1846; *Omoo*, in 1847; *Mardi* and *Redburn*, in 1849; *White-Jacket*, in 1850;

Moby-Dick, in 1851; and *Pierre*, in 1852. During the second period of thirty-eight years, Melville published *Israel Potter*, in 1855; *The Piazza Tales*, in 1856; *The Confidence Man*, in 1857; *Battle-Pieces*, nine years later, in 1866; *Clarel*, ten years later, in 1876; *John Marr*, twelve years later, in 1888; and *Timoleon*, in 1891; the last four being volumes of verse.

To the collector, and bibliographer, of Melville, the year 1853 marks not only the close of his series of great novels, and the dawn of that long half-light of unpopularity superinduced by the appearance of the disastrous *Pierre;* it marks also the occasion of a physical disaster which renders the books published by him in America prior to that date even more scarce today than would normally have been the case.

At one o'clock on the afternoon of Saturday, December 10, 1853, the establishment of Melville's publishers, Harper Brothers, on Franklin Square and Cliff Street, was completely destroyed by fire, supposed to have originated in the throwing by a plumber of a lighted taper into a bucket of camphene, mistaken by him for water.

The event is reported as follows in the *New York Tribune* for Monday, December 12, 1853:

NARRATIVE

OF A

FOUR MONTHS' RESIDENCE

AMONG THE NATIVES OF A VALLEY OF

THE MARQUESAS ISLANDS;

OR,

A PEEP AT POLYNESIAN LIFE.

By HERMAN MELVILLE.

———————

LONDON:

JOHN MURRAY, ALBEMARLE STREET.

1846.

"Destructive Conflagration.
Harpers' Establishment in Ruins.
Sixteen Buildings Consumed.
Loss of $1,600,000.

"The most alarming fire that has visited our city since the terrific conflagration of 1845 occurred on Saturday afternoon in Cliff and Pearl Streets and Franklin Square, and within a few hours the immense Book Publishing House of Messrs. Harper and Brothers together with other buildings were a mass of smouldering ruins. . . ."

The Harpers' loss was estimated at $1,400,000; $400,000 in buildings, the remainder in presses, type, etc. The buildings fronting on Cliff Street were entirely destroyed; three other buildings at the corner of Cliff and Ferry Streets escaped any damage whatever.

It has been sometimes stated that the *plates* of Melville's books were destroyed in this fire. This is not the case. An editorial in the same issue of the *Tribune* says:

"The Great Fire.

"A more signal calamity has never fallen upon a private business house than the terrible conflagration of Saturday, by which the extensive publishing establishment of Messrs.

Harper and Brothers was, within the short space of two hours, converted into a heap of smouldering ruins. The fire was terrific in its rapidity. . . .

"The vast property on Franklin Square and Cliff Street, we understand, amounted to nearly $2,000,000, including the buildings, printing apparatus, stereotype plates and the large stock of publications issued by Harper and Brothers. Of this, the stereotype plates, which were kept in underground vaults, are all which have escaped destruction.

"The destruction of important works of literature . . . is extensive and disastrous in the extreme. . . . These are all swept away before the relentless element. The plates, however, are preserved. . . ."

The statement is confirmed by other papers, and by *The Literary World*. But the question of the preservation of the plates is relatively unimportant at present. The collector will be more interested in the fate of the stock of Melville books stored at Harpers' at the time of the fire. From Mr. Weaver's *Herman Melville* one learns that the following copies of Melville's books were destroyed in the fire: *Typee*, 185; *Omoo*, 276; *Mardi*, 491; *Redburn*, 296; *White-Jacket*, 292; *Moby-Dick*, 297; *Pierre*, 494. One is struck at once by the preponderance of copies of *Mardi* and *Pierre* in stock, these being Melville's two least successful works.

From the same source one learns that the following copies were saved: *Mardi*, 10; *Moby-Dick*, 60; *Pierre*, 110.

The first editions involved in the fire seem to have been those of *Mardi* (1849), *White-Jacket* (1850), *Moby-Dick* (1851), and *Pierre* (1852). Of these, *Pierre* was an utter failure, and presumably achieved only a very small sale before the fire, which makes of it unquestionably the scarcest first edition of those published prior to 1853. Collectors are reminded, however, that copies of *Pierre* sold in England were not printed in London, but the sheets were imported from America and issued in a different binding with an English cancel title.

The next in point of scarcity, of the books published in America prior to 1853, is undoubtedly *Typee* in its original form, without the Sequel and with the Appendix; it having been superseded in a few months by a revised, and heavily expurgated, edition. A close third must be *Mardi*.

Of the books published after 1853, the two most scarce are *John Marr* and *Timoleon*, they having been published privately and in limited editions of 25 copies each. The next in point of scarcity is *Clarel*.

An attempt has been made in this Bibliography to give a description of all Melville first editions,

[99]

both American and English, together with a brief historical note, and also as full a list as possible of subsequent reprintings, although the latter is of necessity only tentative, owing to the conflicting information available, and owing to the scarcity of the books themselves, which renders them difficult of examination in unaltered form. This is particularly true of the various issues of *Typee, Omoo,* and *Israel Potter.* A list is also included of the lectures delivered by Melville, and of his magazine and kindred contributions, some of which, it is believed, have escaped attention heretofore.

The compiler of this Bibliography will welcome all corrections and additional information which its appearance may evoke. He also wishes to express his thanks for their courtesy and coöperation to Harper and Brothers; Putnam's; the London publishing houses of Murray, and Routledge; the authorities of the Library of Congress, the Library of the British Museum, the New York Public Library and the Yale University Library; and to Mr. Byrne Hackett and Mr. John C. C. Fletcher of the Brick Row Book Shop, Inc.

Frequent references have been made to Mr. Weaver's *Herman Melville, Mariner and Mystic,* and to Mr. Sadleir's *Excursions in Victorian Bibliography.*

M. M.

May 5, 1922.

I

TYPEE

New York, 1846

TYPEE: / A Peep at Polynesian Life. / Dur-
ing a / Four Months' Residence / in / A
Valley of the Marquesas / with notices of the
French occupation of Tahiti and / the provisional
cession of the Sandwich / Islands to Lord Pau-
let. / By Herman Melville. / Part I. / New
York: / Wiley and Putnam. / London: / John
Murray, Albemarle Street / 1846.

Collation. 12mo, pp. xv +325. Consisting of
half-title = Wiley & Putnam's / library of / American Books. / Typee: / A Peep at Polynesian
Life. / Part I., bearing on reverse a page of
"Recently Published by Wiley and Putnam";
blank page not included in the pagination, bearing on reverse a map of the Marquesas Islands;
title-page; reverse, note of date of entry = 1846,
and at bottom imprint = R. Craighead's Power
Press, / 112 Fulton Street., and = T. B. Smith,
Stereotyper / 216 William Street.; dedication =
To / Lemuel Shaw, / Chief Justice of the Commonwealth of Massachusetts, / this little work is

gratefully inscribed by / The Author., reverse blank; preface, pp. [vii]-ix, reverse blank; contents, pp. [xi]-xv, reverse blank; text, pp. [1] (heading Residence in the Marquesas) to 166, marked End of Part I. Half-title, same as Part I, except states Part II, bearing on reverse a page of "Now Publishing by Wiley and Putnam," dated March 1846; title-page, same as Part I except states Part II, reverse same as Part I. These half-title and title-pages not included in the pagination. Text, pp. [167] (heading Residence in the Marquesas) to 320; followed by Appendix, pp. [321]-325, marked The End, reverse blank; followed by pp. [v]-viii of publishers' announcements.

The book is bound in blue muslin stamped on both covers with same conventional design. On back in gold = Library / of / American / Books / Typee / Herman / Melville / Wiley & Putnam.

The published price was $1.00; paper, 75 cents.

Words Hawaii, Hawaiian, etc., seem to be spelled without second *a* throughout.

The paper parts were bound in yellow paper. On front cover, in black, in double frame = *"Sundry citizens of this good land, meaning well, and hoping well, / prompted by a certain something in their nature, have trained them- / selves to do service in various Essays, Poems, Histories, and books of / Art, Fancy, and Truth."* / Address of the American Copyright Club. / Wiley and Put-

nam's / Library of American Books. / No. XIII.
(XIV.) / Typee: / A / Residence in the Mar-
quesas. / By Herman Melville. / In Two Parts—
Part I. (II.) / New York and London. / Wiley
and Putnam, 161 Broadway = 6 Waterloo Place.
/ *Price, Thirty-seven and a half cents.*

Inside front cover, yellow, announcement of
Wiley and Putnam's Library of American Books,
continued on inside rear cover, yellow. Outside
rear cover, announcement of Wiley and Putnam's
Library of New Books. On Back = Typee. Part
I. (II.), printed from top to bottom.

MELVILLE'S MARQUESAS ISLANDS

London, 1846

Narrative / of a / Four Months' Residence /
among the natives of a valley of / The Marquesas Islands; / or, / A Peep At Polynesian Life. /
By Herman Melville. / London: / John Murray,
Albemarle Street. / 1846.

Collation. Post 8vo, pp. xvi + 285. Consisting of half-title, The Marquesas Islands; / or, /
A Peep at Polynesian Life., reverse blank; title-
page, reverse bears at bottom imprint = London:
Printed by William Clowes and Sons, Stamford
Street.; dedication = To / Lemuel Shaw, / Chief
Justice of the Commonwealth of Massachusetts, /
this little work is affectionately inscribed / By the
[103]

Author., reverse blank. (*Note,* the American edition says "gratefully inscribed.") Preface, pp. [vii]-ix, reverse blank; contents, pp. [xi]-xvi; blank page not included in pagination, reverse of which bears map of Marquesas Islands; text, pp. [1] (headed = A / Residence in the Marquesas.) to 278; half-title, Appendix, reverse blank, included in pagination; text, pp. [281]-285, reverse of which bears imprint = London: / Printed by William Clowes & Sons, / Stamford Street.; followed by one page, dated March, 1846, announcing Mr. Murray's Select List of Works in General Literature, reverse of which bears a list of Periodicals published by Mr. Murray, followed by pp. [3]-14 of Mr. Murray's List of Books; followed by two pages (15-16) of Mr. Murray's Home and Colonial Library. Page 16, at bottom, bears imprint = Bradbury and Evans, Printers, Whitefriars.

The book is bound in red cloth, stamped with conventional design showing Murray's Colonial & Home Library and monogram M in a circle on both covers. On back, in gold, Colonial / and / Home Library / Vol. / XV / Melville's / Marquesas / Islands / Murray. Yellow end papers.

The published price was six shillings. The book was also issued in two parts in Murray's Home and Colonial Library, presumably in the same form as *Omoo, q.v.* The price was two shillings each.

The words Hawaii, Hawaiian and Hawaiians seem to be spelled without the second *a* throughout.

The manuscript of *Typee* was written in 1845, and bought in London, in December, 1845, by John Murray, who purchased the English rights to print 1000 copies for one hundred pounds. The tale appeared first in two parts in Murray's Home and Colonial Library, Part I, February 26, 1846; Part II, April 1, 1846. Four thousand copies of the first edition of the book were printed.

The American rights were purchased by Wiley and Putnam, after John Murray had agreed to publish the book in England, so that to the London house of John Murray belongs the credit of having first recognized Melville. The tale appeared in book form in 1846 simultaneously in New York and London, being one of the first works to be published in this manner.

The Sequel, containing *The Story of Toby*, was written in July, 1846, and incorporated in the Revised Edition published in the same year. Extracts from the Sequel were also published prior to appearance in book form. In England, John Murray paid an additional fifty pounds for the Sequel, which was first printed as a small pamphlet in an edition of 1250 copies, and subsequently incorporated in the book.

In 1849 Harper Brothers took over the publication of *Typee,* they having become Melville's publishers in 1847 with *Omoo.*

From Mr. Weaver's *Herman Melville* one learns that up to January 1, 1849, 6392 copies of *Typee* had been sold in America, netting Melville $655.91; and in England, up to April 29, 1851, 7437 copies, netting $708.40.

The book contains an account of Melville's own experiences in the Marquesas Islands, during a voyage on which he shipped before the mast on the whaler *Acushnet* which sailed from New Bedford in January, 1841. The Sequel contains the story of the escape from the Valley of Typee of his shipmate, Toby.

The book was translated into several foreign languages, including German (Leipsic, 1846) and Dutch (Haarlem, 1847).

The publishers advertised *Typee* as:

"A new work of novel and romantic interest. It abounds with personal adventure, cannibal banquets, groves of cocoanut, coral reefs, tattooed chiefs and bamboo temples; sunny valleys, planted with bread-fruit trees, carved canoes dancing on the flashing blue waters, savage woodlands guarded by horrible idols, *heathenish rites, and human sacrifices."*

[106]

Some of the contemporary press notices are given below.

New York Mirror. Chateaubriand's Atala is of no softer or more romantic tone—Anacharsis scarce presents us with images more classically exquisite. The style has a careless elegance which suits admirably with the luxurious tropical tone of the narrative, and we cannot read the book without suspecting the author to be at least as well acquainted with the London club-houses as with the forecastle of a merchant-man.

Morning News. *Typee* is a happy hit, whichever way you look at it—whether as travels, romance, poetry or humor. It has a sufficiency of all these to be one of the most agreable, readable books of the day. The peculiarity of the book, to us, is the familiar and town life of the author among a race of naked savages. He goes down every day from his hut to a lounging shed of the chiefs . . . as if he were walking from the Astor House to the saloons of the Racket Club.

Anti-Slavery Standard. The whole narrative [is] more entertaining, not so much for the style as the facts, than Robinson Crusoe. We can honestly say of this book that it is curiously charming, and charmingly instructive.

London Times. Mr. Murray's Library does not furnish us with a more interesting book than this, hardly with a cleverer. It is full of the captivating matter upon which the general reader

battens, and is endued with freshness and originality, to an extent that cannot fail to exhilarate
the most enervated and *blasé* of circulating library
loungers. Enviable Herman! A happier dog it
is impossible to imagine than Herman in the
Typee Valley. To describe a day's existence
would be to tell of the promised joys of the
Mahomedan's paradise. . . . It is introduced to
the English public as authentic, which we by no
means think it to be. We have called Mr. Melville a common sailor; but he is a very uncommon
common sailor, even for America, whose mariners
are better educated than our own. His reading
has been extensive . . . his style throughout is
rather that of an educated literary man than of a
poor outcast working seaman on board of a South
Sea whaler.

London Spectator. A book of great curiosity,
and striking in style of composition. . . . Had
this work been put forward as the production of
an English common sailor, we should have had
some doubts of its authenticity in the absence of
distinct proof. But in the United States it is different. There social opinion does not invest any
employment with discredit; and it seems custom-
ary with young men of respectability to serve
as common seamen, either as a probationership
to the navy or as a mode of seeing life. Cooper
and Dana are examples of this practice.

Revised Edition.

A few months after the original publication of *Typee* in book form a Revised Edition was issued, in America, from which the Appendix was omitted, to which a Sequel was added, and the text of which was considerably altered and censored. In England, the Sequel was added, without other changes, to the second printing of 1000 copies in 1846. The Revised American Edition was also issued in parts.

The alterations in text between the original and revised 1846 editions are given below.

1846 Revised, Preface, p. 10, after last paragraph but one, lacks the following:

"There are a few passages in the ensuing chapters which may be thought to bear rather hard upon a reverend order of men, the account of whose proceedings in different quarters of the globe—transmitted to us through their own hands—very generally, and often very deservedly, receives high commendation. Such passages will be found, however, to be based upon facts admitting of no contradiction, and which have come immediately under the writer's cognisance. The conclusions deduced from these facts are unavoidable, and in stating them the author has been influenced by no feeling of animosity, either to the individuals themselves or to that glorious cause which has not always been served by the proceedings of some of its advocates.

"The great interest with which the important events lately occurring at the Sandwich, Marquesas, and Society Islands, have been regarded in America and England, and indeed throughout the world, will, he trusts, justify a few otherwise unwarrantable digressions."

1846 Revised, Contents, lacks the following headings:

Chapter I = The Marquesas—Adventure of a Missionary's Wife among the Savages—Characteristic Anecdote of the Queen of Nukuheva.

Whole of Chapter III in the original edition is omitted in the revised edition; consisting of following headings = Some account of the late operations of the French at the Marquesas—Prudent conduct of the Admiral—Sensation produced by the arrival of the strangers—The first horse seen by the islanders—Reflections—Miserable subterfuge of the French—Digression concerning Tahiti—Seizure of the island by the Admiral—Spirited conduct of an English lady. There are consequently 33 chapters in the revised edition and 34 in the original.

Chapter III = Invasion of their valley by Por-

ter—Reflections—Glen of Tior—Interview between the old King and the French Admiral.

Chapter XVI = Their enjoyments compared
with those of more enlightened communities—
Comparative wickedness of civilised and unen-
lightened people.

Chapter XXIII = Inaccuracy of certain published accounts of the islands—A Reason—Neglected state of heathenism in the valley.

Chapter XXV = Allusion to His Hawaiian
Majesty—A warning—Some ideas with regard to
the civilisation of the islands—Reference to the
present state of the Hawaiians—Story of a Missionary's wife—Fashionable equipages at Oahu—
Reflections.

Besides the differences in text called for by the
changes in contents noted above, the following
alterations occur. (*Note.* The page reference
is to the revised edition.)

p. 1, after the words "Nothing left us but salt-
horse and sea-biscuit" the original edition says:

> "Oh! ye state-room sailors, who make so
> much ado about a fourteen-days' passage
> across the Atlantic; who so pathetically re-
> late the privations and hardships of the sea,
> where, after a day of breakfasting, lunching,
> dining off five courses, chatting, playing
> whist, and drinking champaign-punch, it was
> your hard lot to be shut up in little cabinets

of mahogany and maple, and sleep for ten hours, with nothing to disturb you but those good-for-nothing tars, shouting and tramping over head—what would ye say to our six months out of sight of land?"

p. 4, after the words "all that we know about them is from a few general narratives," the original edition comments on Porter's *Journal of the Cruise of the U. S. Frigate Essex, in the Pacific, during the late war,* and on Stewart's *A visit to the South Seas* while chaplain of the American sloop of war *Vincennes.*

p. 4, last six lines, beginning "Indeed there is no cluster . . ." do not appear in original edition.

p. 12, last line, after the words "at full length upon the boats," the original edition says:

"What a sight for us bachelor sailors! how avoid so dire a temptation? For who could think of tumbling these artless creatures overboard, when they had swam miles to welcome us?"

p. 13, after the words "every species of riot and debauchery," the original edition says:

"Not the feeblest barrier was interposed between the unholy passions of the crew and their unlimited gratification."

p. 14, first line is lacking in the original edition.

p. 18, second paragraph reads as follows in the original edition:

"I may here state, and on my faith as an honest man, that though more than three years have elapsed since I left this same identical vessel, she still continues in the Pacific, and but a few days since I saw her reported in the papers as having touched at the Sandwich Islands previous to going on the coast of Japan."

p. 21, after the second paragraph, the original edition says:

"I shall never forget the observation of one of our crew as we were passing slowly by the entrance of this bay in our way to Nukuheva. As we stood gazing over the side at the verdant headlands, Ned, pointing with his hand in the direction of the Treacherous Valley, exclaimed 'There—there's Typee. Oh, the bloody cannibals, what a meal they'd make of us if we were to take it into our heads to land! but they say they don't like sailor's flesh, it's too salt. I say, maty, how should you like to be shoved ashore there, eh?' I little thought, as I shuddered at the question, that in the space of a few weeks I should actually be a captive in that self same valley."

p. 43, fourth line from bottom, "in such a place as this," reads "in such an infernal place as this," in the original edition.

pp. 98-99, "I felt somewhat embarrassed by the presence of the female portion of the company, but nevertheless removed my frock, and washed myself down to my waist in the stream," in the original edition reads:

"Somewhat embarrassed by the presence of the female portion of the company, and feeling my cheeks burning with bashful timidity, I formed a primitive basin by joining my hands together, and cooled my blushes in the water it contained; then removing my frock, bent over and washed myself down to my waist in the stream."

p. 99, after the words, "the young girls springing buoyantly into the air," the original edition says "and revealing their naked forms to the waist."

p. 126, after the words "which in their language is denominated aka," the original edition says:

"and most refreshing and agreeable are the juices of the aka, when applied to one's limbs by the soft palms of sweet nymphs, whose bright eyes are beaming upon you with kindness; and"

p. 143, the words "In this frame of mind," read

[114]

in the original edition, "In the altered frame of
mind to which I have referred."
p. 153, after the words "[gam]bolling in pur-
suit," the original edition says:

> "But I was ever partial to what is termed in
> the 'Young Men's Own Book'—'the society
> of virtuous and intelligent young ladies'; and
> in the absence of the mermaids, the amuse-
> ment became dull and insipid."

p. 154, after the words "Fayaway and I reclined
in the stern of the canoe," the original edition says
"on the very best terms possible with one another";
p. 179, after the words "their very eyes, seem to
dance in their heads," the original edition says:

> "In good sooth, they so sway their floating
> forms, arch their necks, toss aloft their
> naked arms, and glide, and swim, and whirl,
> that it was almost too much for a quiet,
> soberminded, modest young man like my-
> self."

p. 179, after the words "when they plume themselves for the dance," the original edition says
"they look like a band of olive colored Sylphides
on the point of taking wing."
p. 200, first paragraph, continues in the original
edition as follows:

"As a religious solemnity, however, it had
not at all corresponded with the horrible descriptions of Polynesian worship which we
have received in some published narratives,
and especially in those accounts of the evan-
gelised islands with which the missionaries
have favored us. Did not the sacred character of these persons render the purity of their
intentions unquestionable, I should certainly
be led to suppose that they had exaggerated
the evils of Paganism, in order to enhance
the merit of their own disinterested labors."

p. 200, the words "Yet, notwithstanding all I observed on this occasion," in the original edition
read "For my own part."
p. 211, after the words "shocked at Kory-Kory's
impiety," the original edition says:

"This anecdote speaks for itself. When one
of the inferior order of natives could show
such contempt for a venerable and decrepit
God of the Groves, what the state of religion
must be among the people in general is easily
to be imagined. In truth I regard the Typees as a back-slidden generation. They
are sunk in religious sloth, and require a
spiritual revival. A long prosperity of
bread-fruit and cocoanuts has rendered them
remiss in the performance of their higher

[116]

obligations. The wood-rot malady is spreading among the idols—the fruit upon their altars is becoming oppressive—the temples themselves need re-thatching—the tattooed clergy are altogether too light-hearted and lazy—and their flocks are going astray."

Note. The above is the "Inference" called for in the chapter heading, and the latter should have been removed in the revised edition.

p. 214, after the words "I had been wonderfully pleased," the original edition says:

"I had observed that even the little intercourse Europeans had carried on with the Nukuheva natives had not failed to leave its traces amongst them. One of the most dreadful curses under which humanity labors had commenced its havocks, and betrayed, as it ever does among the South Sea islanders, the most aggravated symptoms. From this, as from all other foreign inflictions, the yet uncontaminated tenants of the Typee Valley were wholly exempt; and long may they continue so. Better will it be for them for ever to remain the happy and innocent heathens and barbarians that they now are, than, like the wretched inhabitants of the Sandwich Islands, to enjoy the mere name of Christians without experiencing any of the vital operations of true religion, whilst, at the

[117]

same time, they are made the victims of the worst vices and evils of civilisation."

p. 216, after the words "creatures to be lost in that country," there is in the original edition an asterisk referring to a footnote concerning sources. There also follow further references in the text of the original edition to European testimony concerning the beauty of the islanders.
p. 218, after the words "induce respect and obedience," the original edition has a paragraph concerning the civil institutions of the Marquesas.
p. 220, the words "All hail, therefore, Mehevi, King over all the Typees! and long life and prosperity to his tropical majesty! But to be sober again after this loyal burst," read as follows in the original edition:

"All hail, therefore, Mehevi, King of the Cannibal Valley, and long life and prosperity to his Typeean majesty! May Heaven for many a year preserve him, the uncompromising foe of Nukuheva and the French, if a hostile attitude will secure his lovely domain from the remorseless inflictions of South Sea civilisation."

These words follow several paragraphs in the original edition attacking the "republican missionaries of Oahu" for referring to the Hawaiian chieftain as "his gracious majesty" (*i.e.,* the ma-

terial removed from the revised edition when the
chapter heading "An allusion to his Hawaiian
Majesty" was removed).

p. 220, the words "To be sure, there were old
Marheyo and Tinor, who seemed to live together
quite socially, but for all that I had sometimes
observed a comical-looking old gentleman dressed
in a suit of shabby tattooing, who appeared to be
equally at home," read as follows in the original
edition:

> "To be sure, there were old Marheyo and
> Tinor, who seemed to have a sort of nuptial
> understanding with one another; but for all
> that, I had sometimes observed a comical-
> looking old gentleman dressed in a suit of
> shabby tattooing, who had the audacity to
> take various liberties with the lady, and that
> too in the very presence of the old warrior
> her husband, who looked on, as good-
> naturedly as if nothing was happening."

p. 221, after the words "the little fellow had no
triangle on his face," the original edition says
"—but on second thoughts, tattooing is not he-
reditary."

p 221, after the words "was decidedly in her
good graces," the original edition says:

> "I sometimes beheld both him and the chief
> making love at the same time. Is it possible,

[119]

thought I, that the valliant warrior can consent to give up a corner in the thing he loves?"

p. 222, after the words "with any of their number," the original edition says "Married women, to be sure!—I knew better than to offend them."
p. 222, after the words "disposition of the male population," the original edition says:

"Where else, indeed, could such a practice exist, even for a single day?—Imagine a revolution brought about in a Turkish seraglio, and the harem rendered the abode of bearded men, or conceive some beautiful women in our own country running distracted at the sight of her numerous lovers murdering one another before her eyes, out of jealousy for the unequal distribution of her favors!—Heaven defend us from such a state of things!—We are scarcely amiable and forbearing enough to submit to it."

p. 223, after the words "than is usually the case with barbarous people," the original edition says:

"A baneful promiscuous intercourse of the sexes is hereby avoided, and virtue, without being clamorously invoked, is, as it were, unconsciously practised."

The above is followed in the original edition by a paragraph on the marriage tie in Tahiti.

p. 223, the words "But, notwithstanding its existence among them," in the original edition read "Notwithstanding the existence of wedlock among the Typees."

p. 223, after the words "bread-fruit-leaf they usually wore in the rear," the original edition has two paragraphs concerning population.

p. 227, in the original edition the words "There seemed to be no rogues of any kind in Typee" do not occur. The original edition chapter begins instead with a paragraph and a half concerning standards of conduct in Typee—"unparalleled, I will venture to assert, in the most select, refined, and pious associations of mortals in Christendom."

p. 228, the first paragraph reads as follows in the original edition:

"So much for the respect in which 'personal property' is held in Typee; how secure an investment of 'real property' may be, I cannot take upon me to say. Whether the land of the valley was the joint property of its inhabitants, or whether it was parcelled out among a certain number of landed proprietors who allowed everybody to 'squat' and 'poach' as much as he or she pleased, I never could ascertain. At any rate, musty parchments and title deeds there were none on the island; and I am half inclined to believe that its inhabitants hold their broad valleys in fee simple from Nature herself; to have and to hold, as long as grass grows and water runs; or until their French visitors, by summary mode of conveyancing, shall appropriate them to their own benefit and behoof."

p. 229, after the words "wealth of the people of Typee," the original edition has two paragraphs concerning the social condition of the Typees.

p. 229, the words "They lived in great harmony with each other," in the original edition read "They showed this spirit of unanimity in every action of life: everything was done in concert and good fellowship."

p. 238, the words "There were some curious looking dogs in the Valley," in the original edition read:

"I think I must enlighten the reader a little about the natural history of the valley.

"Whence in the name of Count Buffon and Baron Cuvier, came those dogs that I saw in Typee?"

p. 239, the words "monstrous imps that tormented some of the olden saints!", in the original edition read "monstrous imps that torment some of Tenier's saints!"

p. 256, the original edition has an additional paragraph concerning Hawaiian dialects.

p. 266, in the original edition the words "to conceal every trace of it," are followed by three paragraphs concerning cannibalism and in particular Captain Cook's big toe. The words "But to my story" do not appear in the original edition.
p. 283, the words "pronounced one expressive English word I had taught him—Home," in the original edition read "pronounced the only two English words I had taught him—Home and Mother."
p. 286, the words "sobbing convulsively," in the original edition read "sobbing indignantly."
p. 286, the words "in doing which he would fain have taken hold of me," in the original edition read "with a rapid gesture which was equivalent to a Deed of Gift."

———

The title-page of the Revised Edition reads:

Typee: / A peep at Polynesian life. / During a/ Four Months' Residence / in / A Valley of the Marquesas; / The revised edition, with a sequel. / By Herman Melville. / Part I. / New York: / Wiley and Putnam. / London: / John Murray, Albemarle Street / 1846.

The title-page of the 1849 edition, the first published by Harpers, reads:

Typee: / A Peep at Polynesian Life, / during a / Four Months' Residence / in / A Valley of the Marquesas; / the revised edition, with a sequel. / By Herman Melville. / New York: / Harper & Brothers, Publishers. / London: John Murray. / 1849.

The Revised Edition contains an additional "Preface to the Revised Edition."

———————

The Revised Edition was reprinted in the following years:

New York: Wiley and Putnam, 1847; Harpers, 1849 (new copyright, printed from original plates); 1850; 1855; 1857; 1865; 1871; 1876; Arthur Stedman, Ed., 1892; 1896; W. Clark Russell, Ed., 1904; Ernest Rhys, Ed., 1907; W. Clark Russell, Ed., 1911; A. L. Sterling, Ed., 1920; Ernest Rhys, Ed., 1921.

Boston: Arthur Stedman, Ed., 1900; 1910; 1919; W. P. Trent, Ed., 1902.

London: John Murray, 1847 (1000 copies); 1848 (1000 copies); 1850; 1855 (750 copies); 1861; 1866; 1877 (500 copies); 1893 (1000 copies); Routledge, 1855 (6000 copies); 1910; H. S. Salt, Ed., 1892; 1898, 1899; W. P. Trent, Ed., 1903; W. Clark Russell, Ed., 1904; 1910; Ernest Rhys, Ed., 1907; 1921.

II

OMOO

New York, 1847

Omoo: / A Narrative of Adventures / *in the* / South Seas. / *By Herman Melville,* / author of "Typee." / *New York:* / Harper & Brothers, Publishers. / *London: John Murray* / 1847.

Note. Lines in italics are printed red.

Collation. 12mo, xv + [17]-389. Consisting of half-title = Omoo. in red, reverse blank; followed by blank page pasted in, reverse of which bears map of South Seas and explanatory note, included in pagination; title-page; reverse, note of date of entry = one thousand eight hundred and forty-seven; dedication = To / Herman Gansevoort, / of Gansevoort, Saratoga County, New York, / This Work / Is cordially inscribed / by his nephew, / The Author. (last line is not centered); reverse blank; preface, pp. [ix]-xii; contents, pp. [xiii]-xv, reverse blank; introduction (headed = Adventures in the South Seas.), p. [17]; text, pp. 18-389. Reverse of p. 389 is blank and is followed by pp. [xv]-xxiii of publishers' notices for *Typee, Revised Edition.* Reverse of p. xxiii is blank, followed by pp. [1]-16 of Harpers' "Valuable New Publications."

(*Note.* Bottom p. 196 = End of Part I. P. 197 = Part II.)

The published price was as follows:

In the Harper Catalog for 1847 the book was advertised: "Muslin $1.25, paper $1.00." In 1849 Harper advertised: "In two parts 50 cents each, or complete in muslin gilt $1.25."

The following typographical errors noted:

p. x, last line, last word, period lacking.

p. 43, heading, Hannmaanoo should be Hannamanoo.

p. 61, heading, period lacking.

p. 130, heading, second word, broken N.

p. 147, last line, last word, hyphen lacking.

p. 330, last line, last word, period lacking.

The book is bound in muslin stamped on both covers with same conventional design of flowers, etc., and bears in center of front cover two sailing vessels and a rowboat at sea, in gold. On back in gold = Omoo. / Melville. / New-York. / Harper & Brothers., and a conventional design of flowers, etc., in gold.

As to the color of the binding, the book was reprinted four times in the same year. In the Gansevoort-Lansing collection in the New York Public Library, there are two copies of *Omoo* identical in every respect except as follows: One, bound in blue watered muslin and the other bound in black pockmarked cloth, with mottled end papers. The red type in the latter is of a lighter shade than that used in the former. As the red type of the third printing is similar to that of the black bound edition, it is advanced tentatively that the blue watered muslin binding is that of the first printing, and the black pockmarked binding that of the second printing.

The third printing is identical with the first except that the title-page bears the words Third Edition, after "author of . . ."; the reverse of p. xxiii in the rear bears a notice of Harpers' new catalogue dated January, 1847; the gold ships are missing from the cover of the binding, which is in black stamped muslin; and the following additional errors noted:

p. 84, fifth l. from bottom, last word, one quotation mark lacking.

p. 260, heading, period lacking.

p. 265, tenth l. from bottom, fourth word partly obliterated.

p. 265, eleventh l. from bottom, second and third words partly obliterated.

p. 265, twelfth line from bottom, h obliterated in "the."

p. 265, signature, M, broken.

The title-pages of the fourth and fifth printings bear the words Fourth Edition, and Fifth Edition, respectively.

[127]

Paper parts, 2 volumes, 12mo, bound in yellow paper. On front cover, in black, in double frame, at top left-hand corner = Part I. (Part II.) ; at top right-hand corner = 50 cents. Below = Omoo: / A Narrative of Adventures / in the / South Seas. / By Herman Melville, / author of "Typee." / Complete in Two Parts. / New York: / Harper & Brothers, Publishers. / London: John Murray. / 1847. Inside front and rear covers white and blank. Rear cover (Part I), announcement of "Works of Sterling Value," (Part II), "Valuable Sterling Productions." On back = Omoo, Part I. (II.), printed from top to bottom.

OMOO

London, 1847

Omoo: / a / Narrative of Adventures / in the / South Seas; / being a sequel to / The "Residence in the Marquesas Islands." / By Herman Melville, / author of "Typee." / London: / John Murray, Albemarle Street: / 1847.

Collation. Post 8vo, pp. xiii + 321. Consisting of blank page, reverse of which bears map of the South Seas and explanatory note; title-page, reverse of which bears at bottom imprint = London: / Spottiswood and Shaw, / New-street-

Square.; dedication, same as New York edition
except all lines are centered; reverse blank; preface, pp. [vii]-ix, dated New York, January 28,
1847, reverse blank; contents, pp. [xi]-xiii, reverse blank; text, pp. [1] (headed Adventures
in the South Seas) to 155, bottom of which is
marked = End of Part I., and 157 (headed =
Part II) to 321, reverse of which bears imprint
same as reverse of title-page. There follow pp.
[1]-4 of announcements of "Mr. Murray's Home
and Colonial Library," one item of which on p. 4
is "The Marquesas, by Hermann (!) Melville."
There follow pp. 5-16 of "Mr. Murray's List of
Books"; bottom of p. 16 bears imprint = Bradbury and Evans, printers, Whitefriars.

The book is bound in red cloth, stamped with
conventional design. On back in gold: Adventures in the South Seas—Murray. Yellow end
papers.

The published price was six shillings, and in
parts, half a crown.

The paper parts did not contain the map.

Bound in greenish paper. On front cover, in
black, in double frame, in top left-hand corner,
No. XLIII (XLIV) ; below = Cheap Literature
for all Classes. / Murray's / Home and Colonial
Library. / Omoo: / or / Adventures In The
South Seas. / Part I. (II.) / London: / John
Murray, Albemarle Street. / *Price Half-a-Crown.*

/ W. Clowes and Sons, Stamford Street. Inside front cover bears list of "New Editions of Standard Works." On back = Melville's South Seas.—Part I. (II.) printed from bottom to top.

The manuscript of *Omoo* was written in 1846, and the tale was published in March, 1847. In England, John Murray paid one hundred and fifty pounds for the copyright. Together with *Typee*, *Omoo* was one of the earliest works to be published simultaneously in New York and London. The first English edition consisted of 4000 copies.

The following extracts from *Omoo*, "The French priests pay their respects," and "A dinner party in Imeeo" appeared in *The Literary World*, April 24, 1847.

The book contains an account of Melville's own experiences in the South Sea Islands, after his rescue from the Valley of Typee by an Australian whaler, in 1842.

The book was translated into German (Leipsic, 1847).

The publishers advertised *Omoo* as follows:

"This work forms the true sequel and counterpart of the author's popular production— *Typee*. The adventures in the present volume embrace both sea and land. The Nautical incidents of the book are extremely interesting, and the Rambles and Excursions on the Islands of Tahiti and Imeeo, most romantic and extraordinary. With respect to *Typee, Omoo* is the reverse of the medal: as the former work presents the only account ever given of the state of nature in which the Polynesians are originally found, so the latter production will exhibit them as affected by a prolonged intercourse with foreigners."

Some of the contemporary press notices are given below.

Douglas Jerrold's Magazine. A stirring narrative of very pleasant reading. It possesses much of the charm that has made Robinson Crusoe immortal.

New York Express. We scarcely remember anything that has emanated from the press, in all respects so perfectly fresh, racy, and charming, as *Omoo.* Like so many gems in one setting, its most pleasant and amusing chapters sparkle upon us . . . these sketches are not unworthy of *Gil Blas* or *Don Quixote.*

Noah's Times. This is really a delightful book, in which one may find food for laughter and sterling information into the bargain. . . . There are portions of the work, infinitely superior to anything of the kind we ever before read.

Albany Spectator. The reputation which *Typee* procured for its author will be rendered still more illustrious by *Omoo*. . . . He is *the* great painter of natural life, and relates sea stories with naturalness and great effect.

Columbian Magazine. We give the place of the honor to the most popular of the recent issues of the press. The author of *Typee,* Mr. Herman Melville, has shared, to a certain extent, the good fortune of Mr. Stephens and Lord Byron— that of going to bed at night an unknown personage and finding himself famous when he got up the next morning. *Typee* has been read, we suppose, by every man, woman, and child in the Union, who undertakes to keep pace at all with the march of the current literature; and its fame has gone abroad also to lands beyond the sea.

Some of the notices, however, were not so friendly. *The Eclectic Review,* for instance, had an article which opens:

> "In noticing Mr. Melville's book our object is to show that his statements respecting the Protestant Mission in Tahiti are perversions of the truth, that he is guilty of deliberate and elaborate misrepresentations, and . . . that he is a prejudiced, incompetent, and truthless witness. . . ."

The book was reprinted in the following years: *New York:* Harpers, 1847 (four reprintings); 1855; 1863; 1868; Arthur Stedman, Ed., 1892 (new copyright); 1896; H. Clark Russell, Ed., 1904; 1911; Ernest Rhys, Ed., 1908, 1921.

Boston: Arthur Stedman, Ed., 1900; 1910; 1919.

London: John Murray, 1848 (1000 copies); 1849; 1850; 1861 (1000 copies); 1866; 1877 (500 copies); 1893 (1000 copies); Routledge, 1855 (6000 copies); 1910; H. S. Salt, Ed., 1892; 1893; H. Clark Russell, Ed., 1904; 1911; Ernest Rhys, Ed., 1908; 1921.

III

MARDI

New York, 1849

2 vols.

Volume I.

Mardi: / and / A Voyage Thither. / By Herman Melville. / In two volumes. / Vol. I. / New York: / Harper & Brothers, Publishers, / 82 Cliff Street. / 1849.

Collation. 12mo, pp. xii + [13]-365. Consisting of title-page; reverse bears note of date of entry = one thousand eight hundred and forty-nine; dedication = Dedicated / to / my Brother, / Allan Melville.; reverse blank; preface dated New York, January, 1849, reverse blank; half-title = Mardi, reverse blank; contents Volume I, pp. [ix]-xii; text, pp. [13]-365, of which reverse is blank and bears at bottom = End of Vol. I.

Volume II.

Same title-page as Volume I, except states Volume II.

Collation. 12mo, pp. xii + [9]-387. Consisting of title-page, note of entry date on reverse; half-title = Mardi, reverse blank; contents Volume II, pp. [ix]-xii; text, pp. [9]-387, which is marked The End, and reverse of which is blank. There follow pp. [1]-8 of Harper announcements.

Both volumes are bound in dark brown muslin stamped on both covers with same conventional design showing publishers' monogram in center in a circle. On back in gold = Mardi / And / A Voyage / Thither. / I. (II.) / Publishers' symbol. Yellow end papers.

The published price was $1.75. There was also a paper edition at $1.50.

MARDI

London, 1849

3 vols.

Volume I.

Mardi: / and / A Voyage Thither. / *By Herman Melville.* / Author of "Typee," and "Omoo." / In Three Volumes. / Vol. I. / London: / *Richard Bentley, New Burlington Street.* / 1849.

Note. Words in italics are printed in red.

Collation. Post 8vo, pp. x + 336. Consist-

ing of title-page, bearing on reverse, imprint =
London: / Printed by Schulze and Co., 13, Poland Street.; dedication = Dedicated / to / My
Brother / Allan Melville., reverse blank; contents of the First Volume, pp. [v]-x; text, pp. [1]
(heading = Mardi: / and / A Voyage Thither.)
to 336, bottom of which says End of Vol. I., and
bears imprint = London: / Printed by Schulze
and Co., 13, Poland Street.

Volume II.

Same title-page as Vol. I., except says Vol. II.
Collation. Post 8vo, pp. x + 335. Consisting of half-title = Mardi. / Vol. II., reverse
blank; title-page, reverse same as Vol. I; contents
of the Second Volume, pp. [v]-x; text, pp. [1]
(same heading as Vol. I.) to 335, bottom of
which says End of Vol. II., and bears imprint =
London: / Printed by Schulze and Co., 13, Poland
Street. Reverse of p. 335 is blank.

Volume III.

Same title-page as Vol. I, except says Vol. III.
Collation. Post 8vo, pp. viii + 348. Consisting of half-title = Mardi. / Vol. III., reverse
blank; title-page, reverse same as Vol. I; contents
of the Third Volume, pp. [v]-viii; text, pp. [1]
(same heading as Vol. I) to 348, bottom of which
says The End, and bears imprint = London: /
Printed by Schulze and Co., 13, Poland Street.

The book is bound in pale green cloth stamped on both covers with same conventional design. On back in gold = Mardi, / and a / Voyage / Thither / H. Melville / Vol. I. (II. III.) / London / Bentley. All three volumes have end papers colored blue and white with a design of small circles enclosing flowers. On the inside front and rear covers of all three volumes this design forms a frame for a publishers' notice printed on the end paper. On the inside front covers this notice is for Established Works of General Interest. / History and Biography.; on the inside rear covers for the same, Voyages and Travels. The bottom of each notice reads London: Richard Bentley, / Publisher in Ordinary to Her Majesty.

The published price was 31 shillings and 6d.

The following typographical errors are noted:

Vol. I., p. 161, heading, XIPHIUS, X and S wrong font.

p. 223, l. 5, l missing in look.

Vol. II., p. 3, numeral missing.

p. 109, numeral given is 113.

p. 294, numeral, broken 4.

p. 334, fifth line from bottom, quotation marks lacking before Let.

Vol. III., p. 315, numeral, broken 5.

The tale appeared on March 16, 1849, in London (1000 copies), and on April 14, 1849, in

New York. It was the first Melville book published in England by Bentley.

Mr. Weaver, in his *Herman Melville*, states that up to February 22, 1850, 2154 copies were sold.

The following extracts from *Mardi*, "Taji sits down to dinner with five-and-twenty kings," and "Sharks and other sea fellows," appeared in *The Literary World*, the former on April 7, 1849, the latter on June 16, 1849.

Some contemporary press notices of *Mardi* are given below.

Revue des Deux Mondes, Paris (translated). A work such as was never heard of before. . . . *Mardi* is the modern political world. This part is the most piquant of the book. The colossal machine invented by Mr. Melville might be compared to the American Panorama now placarded on the walls of London in these terms:

> "Gigantic original American Panorama, now on exhibition in the great American Hall; the prodigious moving Panorama of the Gulf of Mexico, the Falls of St. Anthony, and of the Mississippi, covering an extent of canvass four miles long, and representing more than 4000 miles of scenery."

London Literary Gazette. *Mardi* has posed us. It has struck our head like one of those blows which set every thing dancing and glancing before your eyes like splintered sun's rays. The pages are brilliant; the adventures superb.

Democratic Review. A sort of retina picture, or inverted view of the world, under the name of *Mardi.* *Typee* and *Omoo* are to this work as a seven-by-nine sketch of a sylvan lake with a lone hunter, or a boy fishing, compared with the cartoons of Raphael.

London Examiner. Charles Lamb might have imagined such a party as Mr. Melville imagines at Plato's table.

The book was also severely criticised:

Blackwood's Magazine. Sadly were we disgusted on a persusal of a rubbishing rhapsody entitled *Mardi, and a Voyage Thither.* . . . Why, what trash is this?—mingled, too, with attempts at a Rabelaisian vein, and with strainings at smartness, the style of the whole being affected, pedantic, and wearisome exceedingly. . . . Mr. Melville has evidently written his unintelligible novel to try the public's patience.

Dublin University Magazine. It is, in our estimation, one of the saddest, most melancholy, most deplorable, and humiliating perversions of genius of a high order in the English language.

The book was reprinted in the following years: *New York:* Harpers, 1855; 1864.

IV

REDBURN

New York, 1849

Redburn: / His First Voyage. / Being the Sailor-boy Confessions and Remin- / iscences of the Son-of-a-Gentleman, in / the Merchant Service. / By Herman Melville, / author of "Typee," "Omoo," and "Mardi." / New York: / Harper & Brothers, Publishers, / 82 Cliff Street. / 1849.

Collation. 12mo, pp. xi + 13-390. Consisting of title-page, reverse bears note of date of entry one thousand eight hundred and forty-nine; dedication =To / My younger brother, / Thomas Melville, / now a sailor on a voyage to China, / this Volume is Inscribed. (*Note,* the "To" is not centered), reverse blank; contents, pp. [v]-xi, reverse blank; text, pp. [13]-390. There follow 4 pp. of Harper announcements, of which the first three are of *Typee, Mardi,* and *Omoo;* followed by pp. [1]-11 of Harper "Book List of the present season" dated October, 1849, the first item of which is *Redburn.* Reverse of p. 11 is numbered 14 and is a continuation of the book list. There follow pp. [1]-2 of Harper "Standard Illustrated Works."

The book is bound in brown muslin, stamped on both covers with same conventional design enclosing publishers' monogram in center in a circle. On back in gold = Redburn. / Melville / New York / Harper & Brothers. Yellow end papers.

The published price was $1.00, and in paper 75 cents.

The following typographical errors noted:

p. 45, third l. from bottom, quotation marks omitted after second word.

p. 53, l. 5, Narrows, broken N.

p. 127, l. 12, last word, hyphen lacking.

p. 152, chapter heading, furnituer should be furniture.

p. 279, last line, last word, period lacking.

p. 290, seventh l. from bottom, Seutonius, should be Suetonius.

p. 380, l. 16, last word, period lacking.

p. 383, l. 21, quotation marks at beginning of line should not appear.

REDBURN

London, 1849

2 vols.

Volume I.

Redburn: / His First Voyage. / Being / The Confessions of a Sailor-Boy. / By Herman Melville, / author of "Typee," "Mardi," &c. / In Two Volumes. / Vol. I. / London: / Richard Bentley, New Burlington-Street. / 1849.

Collation. Post 8vo, pp. viii + 316. Consisting of title-page, reverse blank; dedication = To / my younger brother, / Thomas Melville, / now a sailor on a voyage to China, / this volume is inscribed., reverse blank; Contents, pp. [v]-viii; text, pp. [1]-316.

Volume II.

Same title-page as Vol. I, except says Vol. II.

Collation. Post 8vo, pp. viii + 314. Consisting of half-title, Redburn: / His First Voyage. / Vol. II.; reverse bears imprint at bottom = London: / R. Clay, Printer, Bread Street Hill.; title-page, reverse blank; contents, pp. [v]-viii; text, pp. [1]-314, which bears imprint at bottom = R. Clay, Printer, Bread Street Hill.

The two volumes are bound in dark blue cloth,

stamped with conventional design. White end papers with blue pattern, bearing publishers' announcements. The published price was 1 guinea.

The manuscript of *Redburn* was written in New York during the summer of 1849. The tale appeared on August 18, 1849, in New York, and on September 29, 1849, in London (750 copies).

Mr. Weaver, in his *Herman Melville,* states that up to February 22, 1850, 4011 copies were sold.

The following extracts from *Redburn,* "Redburn contemplates making a social call on the Captain," and "A Living Corpse," appeared in *The Literary World,* on November 10, 1849.

The book was translated into German (Grimma, 1850).

Some of the contemporary press notices of *Redburn* are given below.

Albion. Ships and the sea, and those who plow it, with their belongings on shore—these subjects are identified with Herman Melville's name, for he has most unquestionably made them his own. No writer, not even Marryat himself, has observed them more closely or pictured them more impressively.

Boston Post. The book is intensely interesting. The great charm of the work is its realness. It seems to be *fact* word for word. The tale is told simply and without the least pretension; and yet within its bounds are flashes of genuine humor, strokes of pure pathos, and real and original characters.

Noah's Times. The book is in the old vein. It is written for the million, and the million will doubtless be delighted with its racy descriptions of the life of a young sailor.

Philadelphia North American. Herman Melville is one of the few who has made a distinct mark on the literature of his time.

The book was also criticised, as in the following notice:

Dublin University Magazine. It contains some clever chapters, but very much of the matter, especially that portion relative to the adventures of the young sailor in Liverpool, London, etc., is outrageously improbable, and cannot be read with either pleasure or profit. This abortive work . . . neither obtained nor deserved much success. . . .

The book was reprinted in the following years:
New York: Harpers, 1850; 1855; 1863.
London: Bentley, 1853.

REDBURN
OR THE
SCHOOLMASTER OF A MORNING

In closing the subject of *Redburn,* the attention of the reader is invited to a curious volume, described below.

Redburn: / or the / Schoolmaster of a Morning. / New York: / Wm. M. Christie, No. 2, Astor House. / M DCCC XLV.

Collation. 12mo, 71 pp. Consisting of title-page, bearing on reverse note of date of entry, 1844, and at bottom imprint = H. Ludwig, Printer, / Nos. 70 and 72, Vesey-St.; half-title, The Announcement., reverse blank; text, Canto I, pp. [5]-16; half-title, The Arrival., reverse blank; text, Canto II, pp. [19]-34; half-title, The School., reverse blank; text, Canto III, pp. [37]-48; half-title, The Denouement., reverse blank; text, Canto IV, pp. [51]-71. Reverse of p. 71 blank. All half-titles are included in the pagination, and each page, including the blank pages, is enclosed in a frame showing small rosettes at the four corners.

The book is bound in yellow glazed boards, and bears on back Redburn, in black type on paper label pasted on, printed from bottom to top. This binding may have been put on by Mr. Stuart when the book came into his possession. (See below.)

[145]

This volume is to be found in the New York Public Library, in the room devoted to the Stuart collection. In April, 1922, it bore on the title-page, in pencil, a note made by the cataloguer By / Herman Melville. On the same date, among the Herman Melville cards in the general card catalog there appeared a card covering this volume and giving Herman Melville as the author. It is estimated that the cataloguing of this volume was done fully twenty years ago. It is an interesting, and at the same time mortifying, example of the public neglect of Herman Melville, that this card attributing this volume of verse to him should have remained unquestioned during all those years; more especially since, if a genuine Melville, this volume would be his first published book and consequently of considerable interest to biographers.

The book is mentioned in several catalogs, including that of the British Museum, but always anonymously. It is supposed that the cataloguer who made the notation on the title-page looked up *Redburn,* and found Melville given as the author, the reference being of course to the novel.

There are several features of this poem, however, which, if only from the standpoint of coincidence, give it an added and quite unusual interest.

The hero of the poem, and the hero of Melville's novel, are both called Redburn.

The poem was published in 1845, copyright

[146]

1844. Melville was discharged from the Navy, at the close of his *White-Jacket* voyage, in Boston, October, 1844, that is to say, after his visit to Typee. (See below.)

The poem states:

Canto I, p. 5.

"Close where Tioga's hill-side fires
Smoke, dull, above Owego's spires,

*   *   *   *   *

Its front a district school house rears.

*   *   *   *   *

p. 13.

"How, on the morrow would arrive
From great Manhatta's teeming hive

*   *   *   *   *

A pedagogue of likely parts. . . ."

In other words, Redburn in the poem is a schoolmaster. While it is not known that Melville ever taught school in Tioga County, *even temporarily as a substitute,* nevertheless he did teach school in New York State between the years 1837-1840, after his return from Liverpool on the voyage described subsequently (1849) in his novel *Redburn.*

The poem continues:

p. 15.

> "She, conscious that she knew the truth,
> That the new teacher was a youth
> On the wide world an orphan thrown
> To meet its buffetings alone,

p. 16.

> And for his service he would share
> In turn the farmer's homely fare
> With some small pay beside. . . ."

At the time when he taught school Melville's father was dead, and he had already met the buffetings of the wide world during his voyage to Liverpool. Also during his career as a schoolteacher it is known that Melville received a very small stipend, and boarded with the neighboring farmers in rotation.

The poem continues:

Canto II, p. 24.

> "All forward pressed, eager to see
> What sort of teacher it might be—
> And when, as stopp'd the coach, a bound
> Brought the schoolmaster to the ground,
> A murmur of surprise went round.
> 'Twas no old wretch, whose sullen looks
> Told but of punishment and books—

But a fair youth, whose eye of blue
The light of anger never knew.

* * * * *

Canto III, p. 47.

"The damsels smiling, thought the swain
Well might adorn the suitor train,
And lightly laughed at punishment
When beau and pedagogue were blent;

p. 48.

And the glad urchins, with sly wink,
Curled a contemptuous lip to think
How much a teacher should be feared
Whose chin scarce darken'd with a beard.
. . . ."

Redburn of the poem, therefore, was a very young man, of prepossessing appearance. Melville taught school between the ages of *eighteen and twenty*, and is known to have been of a striking appearance.

The poem continues:

Canto IV, p. 52.

"He [Redburn] dreamed—and thoughts of
    other days
Came o'er his soul like sunny rays.

* * * * *

p. 53.

And now his vision seem'd to change,
And all was beautifully strange.
Far as the eye could reach, was spread
A vale, fit for the fairies' tread;
Upon its arbours grew such fruit
The fairies' dainty taste might suit,
And every leaf and every flower
Might deck a fairy's nuptial bower.
Through the bright valley flow'd a stream,
Where, 'twixt the trees, the sun would gleam
And kiss the wave in laughing play,
Though jealous leaves would often stray
To keep him from the foam away."

It is difficult not to turn at once to Melville's descriptions of the Valley of Typee, in the Revised Edition, where he says:

pp. 46-47. "From the spot where I lay . . . I looked straight down into the bosom of a valley, which swept away in long wavy undulations to the blue waters in the distance. . . . Everywhere below me . . . the surface of the vale presented a mass of foliage, spread with such rich profusion, that it was impossible to determine of what description of trees it consisted.

"But perhaps there was nothing about the scenery I beheld more impressive than those silent cascades, whose slender threads of water . . . were lost amidst the rich herbage of the valley.

"Over all the landscape there reigned the most hushed repose, which I almost feared to break, lest, like the enchanted gardens in the fairy tale, a single syllable might dissolve the spell."

p. 57. "So glorious a valley—such forests of bread-fruit trees—such groves of cocoa-nut — such wildernesses of guava bushes!"

p. 67. "That magnificent vale. . . ."

p. 68. "We followed the course of the stream. . . ."

p. 69. "We descried a number of trees . . . which bear a most delicious fruit. . . ."

Fortunately for the peace of mind of the reader, the remainder of the poem *Redburn* is free from apparent allusions to the author of the novel *Redburn*.

V

WHITE-JACKET

New York, 1850

White-Jacket; / or / The World In a Man-Of-War. / By Herman Melville, / author of "Typee," "Omoo," "Mardi," and "Redburn." / New York: / Harper & Brothers, Publishers, / 82 Cliff Street. / London: Richard Bentley. / 1850.

Collation. 12mo, pp. vii + [9]-465. Consisting of title-page, reverse bears note of date of entry, one thousand eight hundred and fifty; quotation from Fuller's "Good Sea-Captain," reverse bears author's note, dated New York, March, 1850; contents, pp. [v]-vii, reverse of which is blank; text, pp. [9] (headed White-Jacket) to 462; pp. [463]-465 contain unnumbered chapter entitled The End, not included in Contents. Reverse of p. 465 is blank. There follow six unnumbered pages of publishers' announcements, the first four of which are of *Redburn, Mardi, Omoo,* and *Typee.*

The book is bound in brown cloth, stamped

with same conventional design on both covers, bearing the words Harper and Brothers New York in center. On back, in gold, White-Jacket. / Melville. / New York. / Harper & Brothers. Yellow end papers.

The published price was $1.25.

The book was also issued in two parts bound in paper.

Part I.

Collation. 12mo, pp. vii + [9]-240. Consisting of title-page, reverse bears note of date of entry, one thousand eight hundred and fifty; author's note, dated New York, March, 1850, reverse bears quotation from Fuller's "Good Sea-Captain"; contents (both parts), pp. [v]-vii, reverse of which is blank; text, pp. [9]-240.

Part II.

Collation. 12mo, pp. [241]-465, consisting only of text. Reverse p. 465 blank, followed by 14 pages of publishers' announcements, first four of which are of *Redburn, Mardi, Omoo,* and *Typee.*

The parts are bound in yellow paper. On front cover, in double frame, in black, top left-hand corner, Part I. (II.), top right-hand corner, 50 cents. In center White-Jacket; / or / The World In A Man-Of-War. / By Herman Melville, / author of "Typee," "Omoo," "Mardi," and "Redburn." / Complete in Two Parts. / New York: / Harper & Brothers, Publishers, / 82 Cliff Street. / 1850. Inside front and rear covers blank. Rear cover, Part I, announcement of "Book List for the present season, May 1850," Part II, "New Books." The published price was 50 cents each part.

WHITE-JACKET

London, 1850

2 vols.

(From "Excursions in Victorian Bibliography," Sadleir.)

White-Jacket: Or The World in a Man of War. By Herman Melville. London: Richard Bentley, New Burlington Street, 1850. 2 vols. Ex. Cr. 8vo (4¾ x 7¾).
Vol. I, pp. vi + 322.
Vol. II, pp. iv + 315 + [1].
No half-titles. Pale blue cloth, gilt, blocked in blind. Yellow end papers, printed with publishers' advertisements. Vol. I, pp. iii and iv, contain a preface dated October, 1849, and different in content from the note on p. iv of the American edition dated March, 1850.

The published price was 21 shillings.

The manuscript was written in New York City during the summer of 1849. In November of that year Melville went to London to dispose of it. Richard Bentley offered two hundred pounds for the English rights to print 1000 copies. The manuscript was refused by Murray, Colbour, and Moxon. Finally, in December, Bentley confirmed his previous offer, and accepted the manuscript for publication at the end of March, 1850 (1000 copies). The American edition is subsequent to the English.

The following extract, "A shore emperor on board a man of war," appeared in *The Literary World,* March 9, 1850.

The book contains an account of Melville's own experiences subsequent to those related in *Omoo,* as a sailor aboard the United States Frigate *United States,* from which he received his discharge in Boston, in October, 1844.

Of this book the *Dublin University Magazine* said:

> "This is, in our opinion, his very best work. . . . Take it all in all, *White-Jacket* is an astonishing production, and contains much writing of the highest order."

The book was reprinted in the following years:
New York: Harper, 1855; Arthur Stedman, Ed., 1892; 1896.

Boston: Arthur Stedman, Ed., 1900; 1910; 1919.

London: 1855; 1892; 1893; 1901.

VI

MOBY-DICK

New York, 1851

Moby-Dick; / or, / The Whale. / By / Herman Melville, / author of / "Typee," "Omoo," "Redburn," "Mardi," "White-Jacket." / New York: / Harper & Brothers, Publishers. / London: Richard Bentley. / 1851.

Collation. 12mo, pp. xxiii + 634. Consisting of title-page, reverse bears note of date of entry, 1851; dedication = In Token / of my admiration for his genius, / This Book Is Inscribed / to / Nathaniel Hawthorne., reverse blank; Contents, pp. [v]-vi; half-title, Moby-Dick; / or, / The Whale., reverse bears note headed Etymology; p. [ix], Etymology, reverse bears note headed Extracts; pp. [xi]-xxiii, Extracts, reverse of p. xxiii blank; text, pp. [1]-634; followed by page containing Epilogue, reverse of which is blank; followed by six pages of publishers' announcements. The book is bound in pale blue cloth, stamped with conventional design. Orange end papers.

The American edition contains thirty-five passages omitted from the English edition.

The published price was $1.50.

THE WHALE

London, 1851

3 vols.

*(From "Excursions in Victorian Bibliography,"
Sadleir.)*

The Whale. By Herman Melville, author of "Typee," "Omoo," "Redburn," "Mardi," "White-Jacket." (Quotation from *Paradise Lost.)* London: Richard Bentley, New Burlington Street. 1851. 3 vols. Ex. Cr. 8vo (4¾ x 7¾).

Vol. I, pp. viii + 312.

Vol. II, pp. iv + 303 + [1].

Vol. III, pp. iv + 328.

Vol. I only has half-title, on which the story is described as The Whale or Moby-Dick.

Quarter cream cloth blocked in gold; bright blue embossed cloth sides, blocked in blind. Pale yellow end papers.

The published price was 31 shillings and 6 pence.

The manuscript was written at Arrowhead, Massachusetts, in 1850-1851. The tale was published in October, 1851. In England Richard Bentley agreed to pay one hundred and fifty pounds for the first 1000 copies, and half profits thereafter. The American edition is subsequent to the English (500 copies).

The following extract, "The Town-Ho's Story," appeared in *Harper's New Monthly Magazine,* October, 1851.

Extracts from press notices are given below.

Dublin University Magazine. It is quite as eccentric and monstrously extravagant in many of its incidents as even *Mardi;* but it is, nevertheless, a very valuable book, on account of the unparalleled mass of information it contains on the subject of the history and capture of the great and terrible cachalot or sperm-whale.

Literary World. Moby-Dick may be pronounced a most remarkable sea-dish—an intellectual chowder of romance, philosophy, natural history, fine writing, good feeling, bad sayings—but over which, in spite of all uncertainties, and in spite of the author himself, predominates his keen perceptive faculties, exhibited in vivid narration.

The book was reprinted in the following years: *New York:* Harper, 1863; Arthur Stedman,

Ed., 1892; 1896. Another edition, 1892; 1899; Ernest Rhys, Ed., 1907; 1921. Dodd Mead, 1922.

Boston: Arthur Stedman, Ed., 1900; 1910; 1919.

London: Bentley, 1853; L. Becke, Ed., 1901; Ernest Rhys, Ed., 1907; 1921. Another edition, 1912; Violet Maynell, Ed., 1920; 1921.

VII

PIERRE

New York, 1852

Pierre; / or, / The Ambiguities. / By / Herman Melville. / New York: / Harper & Brothers, Publishers / 329 & 331 Pearl Street, / Franklin Square. / 1852.

Collation. 12mo, pp. viii + 495. Consisting of title-page, reverse bears note of date of entry, 1852; dedication To / Greylock's Most Excellent Majesty, etc., reverse blank; table of contents, pp. [v]-viii; text, pp. [1]-495, reverse of which is blank.

The book is bound in grey cloth, stamped with conventional design. Grey end papers.

The published price was, cloth $1.25, paper $1.00.

PIERRE

London, 1852

Copies issued in England consist of the American sheets, with a cancel title = Pierre: Or The

Ambiguities. By Herman Melville. London:
Sampson Low Son and Co., 47 Ludgate Hill.
1852. Bound in blue embossed cloth, stamped
with conventional design. Yellow end papers.

The price was 8 shillings and 6 pence.

The manuscript was written at Arrowhead,
Massachusetts, in 1851. The tale was published
in November, 1852.

The book contains much autobiographical material concerning Melville's childhood, and supposed depictions of his parents.

Extracts from contemporary press notices are
given below.

London Men of the Time. An unhealthy, mystic romance. . . . A decided failure. . . .

London Athenaeum. It is one of the most dif-
fuse doses of transcendentalism offered for a long
time to the public. . . . That many readers will
not follow "the moody ways of Pierre" is, in our
apprehension, not amongst the ambiguities of the
age. The present chaotic performance has nothing American about it, except that it reminds us
of a prairie in print, wanting the flowers and
freshness of the savannahs, but almost equally
puzzling to find a way through it.

Literary World. The object of the author,
perhaps, has been, not to delineate life and char-

acter as they are or may possibly be, but as they are not and cannot be. We must receive the book, then, as an eccentricity of the imagination.

The most unmoral *moral* of the story, if it has any moral at all, seems to be the impracticability of virtue. . . .

In commenting upon the vagueness of the book, the uncertainty of its aim, the indefiniteness of its characters, and want of distinctness in its pictures, we are perhaps only proclaiming ourselves as the discoverers of a literary mare's nest, this vagueness, as the title of the "Ambiguities" seems to indicate, having been possibly intended by the author, and the work meant as a problem of impossible solution, to set critics and readers a woolgathering. It is alone intelligible as an unintelligibility.

The book was reprinted by Harper, in 1855.

VIII

ISRAEL POTTER

New York, 1855

Israel Potter: / His Fifty Years of Exile. /
By / Herman Melville, / author of "Typee,"
"Omoo," etc. / New York: / G. P. Putnam & Co.,
10 Park Place. / 1855.

Collation. 12mo, 276 pp. Consisting of title-
page; reverse, note of date of entry = 1855, and
at bottom imprint = Printed and stereotyped by
Billin and Brother, 20 North William St., N. Y.;
dedication, pp. [3]-5, headed To / His High-
ness / the / Bunker Hill Monument., dated June
17, 1854; reverse p. 5 blank; contents, pp. [7]-8;
text, pp. [9] (headed Israel Potter: / Fifty
Years of Exile) to 276.

The book was bound in green cloth, stamped
on both covers with border, and identical conventional design in center enclosing publishers' monogram. On back in gold = Fifty / Years / Exile /
Melville. / Putnam. Yellow end papers.

The published price was 75 cents.

Typographical errors noted:

p. 137, l. 17, Tristam should be Tristram.

p. 276, heading, period should be colon.

The book was reprinted twice in the same year.

The second printing is identical with the first, except that binding is red, and following additional typographical errors noted:

p. 113, l. 1, third word, broken y.

p. 116, l. 3, fifth word, t obliterated.

p. 116, l. 4, fifth word, t obliterated.

p. 119, second line from bottom, seventh word, i missing.

p. 188, heading, colon broken.

p. 201, l. 1, last word, hyphen lacking.

The third printing is identical with the second, except that the binding is brown; the titlepage bears the words Third Edition after "author of . . ."; and following additional typographical errors noted:

p. 122, heading, period should be colon.

p. 183, heading, period lacking.

p. 275, last line, last word, e lacking.

The book was issued in 1865 in Philadelphia under the title of:

THE REFUGEE

The Refugee. / By / Herman Melville. / Author of "Typee," "Omoo," "The Two Captains," "The Man of / the World," etc., etc. /

[165]

"Written with a life-like power. We advise no one
to take up 'The Refugee' / until he has the leisure
to finish it; for when he has once dipped into its
fasci- / nating and adventurous pages, he will not
be disposed to leave them until he has / reached
the very last." / "This is really a delightful book,
in which one may find food for laughter and / sterling information into the bargain. It is written
in a pleasant off-hand style, / such as will be enjoyed by everybody. There are portions of the
work, infinitely / superior to anything of the kind
we ever before read." / Philadelphia: / T. B.
Peterson & Brothers, / 306 Chestnut Street.

Collation. 8vo. Title-page, bearing on reverse note of date of entry = 1865; and text, pp.
19 (heading = The Refugee. / By Herman Melville.) to 286. There is no dedication, and no
table of contents as in Putnam edition.

The book is bound in black pressed cloth, with
double border and conventional design in center
showing publishers' name on both covers. On
back = The / Refugee (in black in a gold panel
stamp) / (in gold) Melville. / Publishers' symbol / T. B. Peterson & Brothers. The whole
enclosed in a gold frame.

The same typographical errors as in the third
printing of the Putnam edition noted, except that
the missing *e* on p. 275 of that edition is corrected
in this one (p. 285). None of the errors in page
headings of the Putnam edition occur, as the page

heading for the 1865 edition is The Refugee throughout.

The published price was, cloth $1.75, paper $1.50.

A copy of *The Refugee,* formerly the property of Melville's cousin, Mrs. Lansing, bears a note in pencil on the title-page to the effect that the publishers of *The Refugee* "assumed the right" to publish it after the expiration of the copyright, and the edition has often been referred to subsequently as a pirated edition. This is not the case, however, as the plates were sold by Putnam to Peterson during the panic of 1857. At the time of the sale the plates were valued at $218.66, the book was out of print, and there was no sheet stock.

An undated clipping from the *New York World,* pasted in the copy mentioned above, voices Melville's legitimate objection, not to the publication of the book by Peterson, but to its publication under a changed title, as follows:

"A Protest from Herman Melville

"To the Editor of the *World*

"Sir: Permit me through your columns to make a disavowal. T. B. Peterson and Brothers, of Philadelphia, include in a late list of their publications 'The Refugee' by Herman Melville.

"I have never written any work by that title.

In connection with that title Peterson Brothers employ my name without authority, and
not withstanding a remonstrance conveyed to
them long ago.

Herman Melville."

The matter is again referred to in a letter from
Melville to Mr. James Billson, reprinted in the
London Nation and Athenaeum for August 13,
1921, as follows:

"April 7th, 1888
New York, 104 East 26th Street.
"My dear Sir . . . As for the 'Two Captains' and 'Man of the World,' they are
books of the air—and I know of none such.
The names appear, though, on the title-
page of a book of mine—'Israel Potter'—
which was republished by a Philadelphia
house some time ago, under the unwarrant-
ably altered title of 'The Refugee.' A letter
to the publisher arrested the publication."

ISRAEL POTTER

London, 1855

*(From "Excursions in Victorian Bibliography,"
Sadleir.)*

Israel Potter: His Fifty Years of Exile. By
Herman Melville, author of "Typee," "Omoo,"
etc. London: G. Routledge and Co., Farring-
ton Street. 1855. 1 Vol. F, cap, 8vo (4 x 6½).
Pp. 174. Bright yellow paper wrappers printed
in black. The outside back wrapper is occupied
by publishers' advertisements. Also issued simultaneously in cloth.

The published price was 1 shilling.

The tale was published in April, 1855, by Putnam, having previously appeared serially in *Putnam's Monthly Magazine,* July, 1854-March,
1855.

The book is based on the *Life and Remarkable
Adventures of Israel R. Potter,* 1824, purporting
to be the true story of a soldier in the American
Revolution, captured by the British at the Battle
of Bunker Hill. Melville's book contains what
are considered able sketches of George III, Dr.
Franklin, Paul Jones, Ethan Allen, and the fight
between the *Bonhomme Richard* and the *Serapis.*

Extracts from contemporary press notices are
given below.

[169]

Hartford Republican. The descriptions with which it abounds are among the finest in the language. Such splendid writing rarely issues. from the press.

London Athenaeum. Mr. Melville's books. have been, from the outset of his career, somewhat singular, and this is not the least so of the company. . . . Mr. Melville tries for power, and command, but he becomes wilder and wilder, and more and more turgid in each successive book.

The book was reprinted in the following years: *New York:* Putnam, 1855 (reprinted twice). *London:* Murray, 1861.

Philadelphia: T. B. Peterson, 1865 (from original plates, with title of *The Refugee*).

IX

THE PIAZZA-TALES

New York, 1856

The / Piazza Tales. / By / Herman Melville, / author of "Typee," "Omoo," etc., etc., etc. / New York; / Dix & Edwards, 321 Broadway. / London: Sampson Low, Son & Co. / 1856.

Collation. 12mo, pp. [iv] + 431. Consisting of title-page, reverse bears note of date of entry, 1856, and imprint = Miller & Holman, / Printers & Stereotypers, N. Y.; contents, reverse blank; text, pp. [1]-29, The Piazza, reverse blank; [31]-107, Bartleby, reverse blank; [109]-270, Benito Cereno; [271]-285, The Lightning-Rod Man, reverse blank; [287]-399, The Encantadas, reverse blank; [401]-431, The Bell-Tower, reverse blank; followed by 7 pages of publishers' announcements.

The book is bound in pale blue cloth, stamped on both covers with same conventional design showing publishers' monogram in an oval of corn-stalks; on back, in gold, enclosed in same design = The / Piazza / Tales / Melville., and at bottom = Dix Edwards & Co. While some copies of the first edition have blue end papers, that owned by Mr. Evert Duyckinck (see Part One of this work) has yellow end papers, and it is reasonable to assume that his copy would have been among the first issued.

The published price was $1.00.

While the book was advertised in England at 9 shillings, and noticed by English reviewers, it is doubtful whether it was ever issued in England.

The book, published in 1856, contains a collection of short tales. The first of these, *The Piazza,* gives an account of Melville's farmhouse at Arrowhead, Massachusetts; the other five had already appeared in *Putnam's Monthly Magazine* as follows:

Bartleby, the Scrivener, November-December, 1853.

The Encantadas, March-May, 1854.

The Lightning-Rod Man, August, 1854.

The Bell Tower, August, 1855.

Benito Cereno, October-December, 1855.

The London *Atlas* mentioned the book as follows:

"Who that remembers those charming works of Mr. Melville, *Typee* and *Omoo,* will not be glad of an opportunity of meeting him on his Piazza, while he recites the delightful stories which are contained in the volume before us?"

The book was never reprinted.

X

THE CONFIDENCE-MAN

New York, 1857

The / Confidence-Man: / His Masquerade. / By / Herman Melville, / author of "Piazza Tales," "Omoo," "Typee," etc., etc. / New York: / Dix, Edwards & Co., 321 Broadway. / 1857.

Collation. 12mo, pp. [vi] + 394. Consisting of title-page; reverse, note of date of entry = 1857, and at bottom imprint of Miller & Holman, / Printers and Stereotypers, N. Y.; contents, pp. [iii]-vi (all lines centered and no page references given); text, pp. [1] (headed The Confidence-Man: / His Masquerade.) to 394.

The book is bound in grcen cloth, stamped on both covers with border, and conventional design in center. On back in gold = The / Confidence / Man / Melville / Dix, Edwards & Co.

The published price was $1.00.

THE CONFIDENCE-MAN

London, 1857

(From "Excursions in Victorian Bibliography," Sadleir.)

The Confidence-Man: His Masquerade By Herman Melville, author of "The Piazza Tales," "Omoo," "Typee," etc., etc. Authorised Edition. London: Longman, Brown, Green, Longmans and Roberts. 1857. 1 Vol. F, cap. 8vo (4¼ x 6¾). Pp. vi + 354. No half-title. Publishers' catalogue, 24 pp., dated September, 1855, bound in at end. Yellow-brown cloth, gilt, blocked in blind. Brick-red end papers, partially printed with publishers' advertisements.

The published price was 5 shillings.

The tale was published in April, 1857. The action takes place aboard a Mississippi river boat, and it would seem to have been the author's intention to write a sequel.

Some contemporary press notices of the book are given below.

Westminster Review. It required close knowledge of the world, and of the Yankee world, to write such a book, and make the satire acute and telling and the scenes not too improbable for the faith given to fiction. Perhaps the moral is, the gullibility of the great Republic when taken on its own tack. . . . Few Americans write so powerfully as Mr. Melville, or in better English; and we shall look forward with pleasure to his promised continuation of the Masquerade. The first part is a remarkable work, and will add to his reputation.

London Leader. The charm of the book is owing to its originality and to its constant flow of descriptions, character sketching, and dialogue, deeply toned and skilfully contrasted.

London Saturday Review. There is one point on which we must speak a serious word to Mr. Melville before parting with him. He is too clever a man to be a profane one; and yet his occasional irreverent use of Scripture phrases in such a book as the one before us gives a disagreeable impression. We hope he will not in future mar his wit and blunt the edge of his satire by such instances of bad taste.

The book was never reprinted.

XI

BATTLE-PIECES

New York, 1866

Battle-Pieces / and / Aspects of the War. / By / Herman Melville. / New York: / Harper & Brothers, Publishers, / Franklin Square. / 1866. *Collation.* 12mo, pp. x + [11]-272. Consisting of title-page; reverse, note of date of entry = one thousand eight "hnndred" and sixty-six; dedication = The Battle-Pieces / in this volume are dedicated / to the memory of the / Three Hundred Thousand / who in the war / for the maintenance of the Union / fell devotedly / under the flag of their fathers; reverse blank; author's note, beginning "With few exceptions, the Pieces in this volume originated in an impulse imparted by the fall of Richmond . . ."; reverse blank; contents, listing 71 poems, pp. [vii]-x; poem, *The Portent* (1859), not included in contents, p. [11]; reverse blank; text, pp. [13]-162; half-title = Verses / Inscriptive and Memorial; reverse blank; text, pp. [165]-[183]; reverse blank; half-title = The Scout toward Aldie; reverse blank; text, pp. [187]-225; reverse blank; half-title = Lee in the Capitol; reverse blank; text, pp. [229]-237; reverse blank; half-title = A Meditation, (etc.); reverse blank; text, pp. [241]-243; reverse blank; half-title = Notes; reverse blank; text, pp. [247]-255; reverse blank; half-title = Supplement; reverse blank; text, pp. [259]-272. All half-titles are included in the pagination. Throughout the book the page on which a poem begins is not numbered. The longest poem included is *The Scout toward Aldie*, 39 pp. The at one time well-known *Sheridan at Cedar Creek* is on pp. 116-117.

The book is bound in blue cloth, bearing publishers' monogram in a circle in center of both covers. On back in gold = Battle / Pieces. / Melville. / Ornament / Harpers. Brown end papers.

The published price was $1.75.

The book was not issued in England.

This volume of verse was published in 1866. Melville states that "with few exceptions, the Pieces in this volume originated in an impulse imparted by the fall of Richmond. . . ."

The volume opens with *The Portent* (1859), not included in the table of contents, and given in full below:

"Hanging from the beam,
  Slowly swaying (such the law),

Gaunt the shadow on your green,
Shenandoah!
The cut is on the crown
(Lo, John Brown),
And the stabs shall heal no more.

"Hidden in the cap
Is the anguish none can draw;
So your future veils its face,
Shenandoah!
But the streaming beard is shown
(Weird John Brown),
The meteor of the war."

Of the poems included in this volume, the following had already appeared in magazines:

"The March to the Sea," *Harper's New Monthly Magazine*, February, 1866.

"The Cumberland," *Harper's New Monthly Magazine*, March, 1866.

"Chattanooga," *Harper's New Monthly Magazine*, June, 1866.

"Gettysburg: July, 1863," *Harper's New Monthly Magazine*, July, 1866.

The book was never reprinted.

XII

CLAREL

New York, 1876

2 vols.

Volume I.

Clarel / a poem / and / pilgrimage in the Holy
Land. / By / Herman Melville / in four parts /
I. Jerusalem III. Mar Saba / II. The Wilder-
ness IV. Bethlehem / Vol. I / New York / G. P.
Putnam's Sons / No. 182 Fifth Avenue / 1876.

Collation. 16mo, pp. 300. Consisting of title-
page, reverse bears copyright note, 1876; dedication, reverse blank, pasted in, not included in
pagination = By / a spontaneous act, / not very
long ago, / my kinsman, the late / Peter Gansevoort, / of Albany, N. Y., / In a personal interview provided for the publica- / tion of this poem,
known to him by report, / as existing in manuscript. / Justly and affectionately the printed book
is / Inscribed With His Name.; contents, 3 pp.,
of which the second and third are numbered ii
and iii, though actually they are 4 and 5; reverse

of p. iii bears author's note; text, Part I, pp. [7]-152; half-title = Part II. / the Wilderness, reverse blank, included in pagination; text, Part II, pp. [155]-300.

Volume II.

Title-page same as Volume I, except says Vol. II.

Collation. 16mo, pp. iv + [301]-571. Consisting of title-page, reverse bears copyright note, 1876; contents, pp. [iii]-iv; half-title, Part III. / Mar Saba., included in pagination, p. [301], reverse blank; text, Part III, pp. [303]-436; half-title, Part IV. / Bethlehem., included in pagination, reverse blank; text, Part IV, pp. [439]-571, reverse of which is blank.

Each volume is bound in brick-red cloth, stamped in gold on front cover only with emblem of palm leaves, crosses, crowns and star. On back, in gold, Clarel / a / Pilgrimage / in the / Holy Land / Melville / I. (II.) / Putnam. Chocolate end papers.

The published price was $3.00.

The book was not issued in England.

These two volumes of verse were published in July, 1876, at the expense of Melville's uncle, Hon. Peter Gansevoort. The manuscript had been in existence for some time.

The poem was inspired by Melville's journey to the Holy Land, in 1856.

The poem was never reprinted.

XIII

JOHN MARR

New York, 1888

John Marr / and other sailors / (*these two lines not centered*) With some sea-pieces / *decoration* / New-York / The De Vinne Press / 1888.

Collation. 16mo, 4 unnumbered pages + pp. 103. Consisting of Title-page, reverse of which bears imprint = Copyright, 1888, by / Theo. L. De Vinne & Co.; Table of Contents, reverse blank; "Inscription epistolary to W. C. R.," etc., pp. [1]-7, reverse of which is blank; half-title, John Marr / and other Sailors., reverse blank; text, pp. 11-23, reverse of which is blank; half-title, Bridegroom Dick, reverse blank; text, pp. 27-50; half-title, Tom Deadlight, reverse blank; text, pp. 53-56; half-title, Jack Roy, reverse blank; text, pp. 59-61, reverse of which is blank; half-title, Sea-Pieces, reverse blank; text, pp. 65-76; half-title, The Aeolian Harp / at the Surf Inn., reverse blank; text, pp. 79-81, reverse of which is blank; half-title, Minor Sea-Pieces., reverse blank; text, pp. 85-97, reverse of which is blank; half-title, Pebbles, reverse blank; text, pp. 101-103, reverse of which is blank. All half-titles included in pagination.

The book is bound in yellow paper. On front cover, in black = (upper left-hand corner) 25 copies (underlined). Remainder of cover as follows = John Marr *decoration* / *decoration* And Other Sailors / With some sea-pieces / *decoration* / New-York / The De Vinne Press / 1888. Other covers blank.

The volume contains 19 poems. The edition was privately printed, and limited to 25 copies. The initials of the Inscription Epistolary stand for W. Clark Russell.

The Princeton University Press is about to issue this volume of verse, under the title of *John Marr and other poems,* edited by Mr. Henry Chapin.

XIV

TIMOLEON

New York, 1891

Timoleon / etc. / *Decoration* / New York /
The Caxton Press / 1891.
Collation. 16mo, pp. vi + [7]-70. Consisting of Title-page, reverse of which bears imprint = Copyright, 1891, by / The Caxton Press;
dedication = To / my countryman / Elihu Ved-
der, reverse blank; Table of Contents, pp. [v]-vi;
text, pp. [7]-15, reverse of which is blank; half-
title, After the Pleasure Party., reverse bears
verse headed Lines Traced under an image of
amor threatening; text, pp. 19-45, reverse of
which is blank; half-title, Fruit of travel long ago;
text, pp. [48]-70; followed by blank leaf. All
half-titles included in pagination.

The book is bound in buff paper. On front
cover in black = Timoleon / etc. / *decoration* /
New York / The Caxton Press / 1891. Other
covers blank.

The volume contains 43 poems. The edition
was privately printed and limited to 25 copies. In

the following poem, quoted from this volume, Melville seems to have summed up his conception of Art:

"In placid hours well pleased we dream
Of many a brave unbodied scheme,
But form to lend, pulsed life create,
What unlike things must meet and mate;
A flame to melt—a wind to freeze;
Sad patience—joyous energies;
Humility—yet pride and scorn;
Instinct and study; love and hate;
Audacity—reverence. These must mate,
And fuse with Jacob's mystic heart,
To wrestle with the angel—Art."

XV

BILLY BUDD

(Unpublished)

Besides ten prose pieces and a body of verse, there still exists in manuscript form a novel, *Billy Budd*, the manuscript of which was completed a short time before Melville's death.

The novel is based on the character of Jack Chase, the captain of the maintop who figures in *White-Jacket,* and is dedicated to him, as follows (quoted from Mr. Weaver's *Herman Melville*):

"To Jack Chase, Englishman, wherever that great heart may now be, Here on earth or harboured in Paradise, ,Captain in the warship in the year 1843, In the U. S. Frigate *United States.*"

XVI

LECTURES

Between 1857 and 1860, Melville sought to increase his income by turning to the lecture platform. J. E. A. Smith says of him that "he did not take very kindly to the lecture platform, but had large and well pleased audiences."

Melville himself, in a letter to George Duyckinck, (Duyckinck collection, New York Public Library) says:

> " . . . if they will pay expenses, and give a reasonable fee, I am ready to lecture in Labrador, or on the Isle of Desolation off Patagonia.
>
> "Bear with mine infirmity of jocularity. . . ."

Mr. Weaver, in his *Herman Melville,* states that Melville had two subjects on which he lectured, *South Seas* and *Statuary in Rome.* He lists the following occasions on which Melville lectured, together with the fee received, described by J. E. A. Smith as "the liberal pay" which lecturers received at that period.

1857-1858

November	24,	Concord, Mass.,	$ 30.00
December	2,	Boston,	40.00
"	10,	Montreal,	50.00
"	30,	New Haven, Conn.,	50.00
January	5,	Auburn, N. Y.,	40.00
"	7,	Ithaca, N. Y.,	50.00
"	10,	Cleveland,	50.00
"	22,	Clarksville,	75.00
?		Chillicothe, O.,	40.00
?		Cincinnati,	50.00
February	10,	Charleston, Mass.,	20.00
"	23,	Rochester, N. Y.,	50.00
?		New Bedford, Mass.,	50.00

$595.00

Travelling expenses,   221.30

$373.70

1858-1859

December	6,	Yonkers, N. Y.,	$ 30.00
"	14,	Pittsfield, Mass.,	50.00
January	31,	Boston,	50.00
February	7,	New York,	55.00
"	8,	Baltimore,	100.00
"	24,	Chicago,	50.00
"	25,	Milwaukee,	50.00
"	28,	Rockford, Ill.,	50.00

[189]

March	2,	Quincy, Ill.,	23.50
"	16,	Lynn, Mass. (2),	60.00
			$518.50

1859-1860

November	7,	Flushing, L. I.,	$ 30.00
February	14,	Danvers, Mass.,	25.00
"	21,	Cambridge, Mass.,	55.00
			$110.00

XVII

CONTRIBUTIONS TO MAGAZINES, ETC.

Fragments from a writing desk, *The Democratic Press and Lansingburgh Advertiser,* May 4, May 18, 1837.

Omoo, extracts, "The French priests pay their respects," and "A dinner party in Imeeo," *Literary World,* April 24, 1847.

Review, Parkman's Oregon Trail, *Literary World,* March 31, 1849.

Review, Cooper's Sea Lions, *Literary World,* April 28, 1849. Melville is also known to have written an article on a new edition of Cooper's Red Rover.

Mardi, extracts, "Taji sits down to dinner with five-and-twenty kings," *Literary World,* April 7, 1849. "Sharks and other sea fellows," *Literary World,* June 16, 1849.

Redburn, extracts, "Redburn contemplates making a social call on the captain," and "A living corpse," *Literary World,* November 10, 1849.

White-Jacket, extract, "A shore emperor on

board a man of war," *Literary World*, March 9, 1850.

Review, Hawthorne's Scarlet Letter, *Literary World*, March 30, 1850.

(*Note*. Besides the reviews already mentioned, there are undoubtedly others by Melville in the *Literary World*, but as they were unsigned they can not now be identified with certainty.)

Hawthorne and his mosses, by a Virginian spending a July in Vermont, *Literary World*, August 17, August 24, 1850.

Moby-Dick, extract, "The Town-Ho's story," *Harper's New Monthly Magazine*, October, 1851.

Article, James Fenimore Cooper, in W. C. Bryant's *A memorial to James Fenimore Cooper*. New York, 1852.

Our young authors, *Putnam's Monthly Magazine*, February, 1853.

Bartleby the Scrivener, a story of Wall Street, *Putnam's Monthly Magazine*, November-December, 1853.

Cock-a-doodle-doo! or the crowing of the cock of Benentano, *Harper's New Monthly Magazine*, December, 1853.

The Encantadas or Enchanted Isles, by Salvator R. Tarnmoor, *Putnam's Monthly Magazine*, March-May, 1854.

The lightning-rod man, *Putnam's Monthly Magazine*, August, 1854.

Poor man's pudding and rich man's crumbs, *Harper's New Monthly Magazine*, June, 1854.

Happy failure, a story of the river Hudson, *Harper's New Monthly Magazine*, July, 1854.

Israel Potter, his fifty years' exile, *Putnam's Monthly Magazine*, July, 1854-March, 1855.

The fiddler, *Putnam's Monthly Magazine*, September, 1854.

Paradise of Bachelors and Tartarus of Maids, *Harper's New Monthly Magazine*, April, 1855.

The bell-tower, *Putnam's Monthly Magazine*, August, 1855.

Benito Cereno, *Putnam's Monthly Magazine*, October-December, 1855.

Jimmy Rose, *Harper's New Monthly Magazine*, November, 1855.

The 'Gees, *Harper's New Monthly Magazine*, March, 1856.

I and My Chimney, *Putnam's Monthly Magazine*, March, 1856.

The apple-tree table, or original spiritual manifestations, *Putnam's Monthly Magazine*, May, 1856.

Poem, The March to the sea, *Harper's New Monthly Magazine*, February, 1866.

Poem, The Cumberland, *Harper's New Monthly Magazine*, March, 1866.

Poem, Philip, *Harper's New Monthly Magazine*, April, 1866.

Poem, Chattanooga, *Harper's New Monthly Magazine*, June, 1866.

Poem, Gettysburg, July, 1863, *Harper's New Monthly Magazine*, July, 1866.

Article, Major Thomas Melville, in J. E. A. Smith's *The History of Pittsfield*, Pittsfield, 1876.